Sophocles
Plays: Two

Ajax, Women of Trachis, Electra, Philoctetes

Sophocles lived through nearly all the Peloponnesian war and his plays are marked by the passion of his characters, many of whom face intolerable pressures which only some manage to survive. Sophocles' plays deal with cause and effect; the loss of honour which leads to suicide, love which provokes destruction, revenge within a family feud – all are concerned with emotional and physical pain. *Ajax* is full of moral paradoxes and problems, and the hero's reversal of fortune, where pride leads to divine punishment. *Women of Trachis* brings together the apparent weakness of a woman too gentle for her own good and the strength of a man too powerful for his. Sophocles' vision of *Electra* focuses on the personal tragedy of the oppressed heroine, on characterisation rather than on the action and again in *Philoctetes* we are drawn into the moral debate over personal loyalty, where public duty is at variance with private conscience. These translations are marked by freshness and clarity making them accessible to scholars and actors alike.

Sophocles was born at Colonus, just outside Athens, the son of a prosperous arms manufacturer. He first won a prize for tragedy in 468 BC, defeating the veteran Aeschylus. Altogether he is said to have composed a hundred and twenty-three plays. His long life spanned the rise and decline of the Athenian Empire and he held several public offices, both military and civil. As a priest of a minor deity he welcomed the cult of Asclepius to Athens in 420 BC, and for this he was honoured as a hero after his death. He was the leader of a fellowship of the Muses, or literary circle, and wrote a prose treatise *On the Chorus*, now lost. He was content to spend all his life at Athens, and is reputed to have refused several invitations to royal courts. When he died, at the age of ninety, Aristophanes testifies that his genial charm was greatly missed.

in the same series

Aeschylus Plays: One
Persians, Seven Against Thebes, Suppliants,
Prometheus Bound

Aeschylus Plays: Two
Oresteia: Agamemnon, Libation-Bearers, Eumenides

Aristophanes Plays: One
Acharnians, Knights, Peace, Lysistrata

Aristophanes Plays: Two
Wasps, Clouds, Birds, Festival Time (*Thesmophoriazousai*),
Frogs

Aristophanes and Menander: New Comedy
Women in Power, Wealth, The Malcontent,
The Woman from Samos

Euripides Plays: One
Medea, The Phoenician Women, Bacchae

Euripides Plays: Two
Hecuba, The Women of Troy, Iphigenia at Aulis, Cyclops

Euripides Plays: Three
Alkestis, Helen, Ion

Euripides Plays: Four
Elektra, Orestes, Iphigeneia in Tauris

Euripides Plays: Five
Andromache, Herakles' Children, Herakles

Euripides Plays: Six
Hippolytos, Suppliants, Rhesos

Sophocles Plays: One (*The Theban Plays*)
Oedipus the King, Oedipus at Colonus, Antigone

SOPHOCLES

Plays: Two

Ajax
translated by Robert Cannon

Women of Trachis
translated by J. Michael Walton

Electra

Philoctetes
translated by Kenneth McLeish

introduced by J. Michael Walton

series editor: J. Michael Walton

METHUEN DRAMA

METHUEN CLASSICAL GREEK DRAMATISTS

3 5 7 9 10 8 6 4

This edition first published in Great Britain in 1990
by Methuen Drama
Reissued in this series with a new cover 1998
by Methuen Drama
Random House, 20 Vauxhall Bridge Road, London SW1V 2SA
and Australia, New Zealand and South Africa

Ajax translation copyright © by Robert Cannon 1990
Women of Trachis translation copyright © by
J. Michael Walton 1990
Electra translation copyright © by Kenneth McLeish 1979, 1990
Philoctetes translation copyright © by Kenneth McLeish 1979, 1990

Introduction copyright © by J. Michael Walton 1990
This collection copyright © by Methuen Drama 1990

The authors and translators have asserted their moral rights

ISBN 0-413-62880-9

Random House UK Limited Reg. No. 954009

A CIP catalogue record for this book
is available from the British Library

Printed and bound in Great Britain by
Cox & Wyman Ltd, Reading, Berkshire

CONTENTS

Introduction   vii

AJAX   1

WOMEN OF TRACHIS   59

Electra and *Philoctetes* –
A Note on the Translation   105

ELECTRA   109

PHILOCTETES   169

A Note on the Translators   227

INTRODUCTION

Sophocles lived to be over ninety. He was a child in Athens during the first and second Persian invasions, repelled by the Athenians at the battles of Marathon in 490 BC and Salamis in 480 BC. After reaching what today is regarded as pensionable age, he was to live through all but the last two years of the twenty-seven year Peloponnesian war in which Athens lost her dignity, her decency and finally her sovereignty. He saw nothing but the fifth century BC, the golden age of Athenian culture, but he saw almost all of it. No prominent Athenian, and certainly no prominent Athenian writer, lived through so much, was involved in so much, both politically and militarily, and survived to refine his experience in the crucible of the theatre of Dionysus.

The reputation that Sophocles enjoyed as a dramatist in his own time was almost unrivalled. The comic playwright Aristophanes, for whom no figure was sacred, has one dig at him in *Peace* for being miserly as he grows old. By the time of *Frogs*, performed sixteen years later in 405 BC in the wake of the recent death of both Sophocles and Euripides, Aristophanes writes Sophocles out of the competition for 'Playwright of the Underworld' by suggesting he was too benign to get involved in such things. A variety of circumstances may have contributed to Aristophanes' decision not to include Sophocles in the contest, but the description of him from Hades as 'amiable up there, amiable down here' carries neither irony nor sarcasm. He was popular as a man and as a playwright, winning first prize at the Great Dionysia on twenty occasions.

In the century following his death Sophocles' plays remained an attraction, regularly revived, if not as often as those of Euripides. When Aristotle came to write the *Poetics*, some seventy years after Sophocles and Euripides died, his purpose was to defend the theatre. Plato had argued in the *Republic* that drama and actors were too dangerous for the ideal state. The earliest critical tribute to Sophocles comes in the *Poetics* when Aristotle praises the construction of his plays and their moral messages in order to justify the existence of theatre.

The problem with such philosophical juggling is that it contrives to make Sophocles sound terminally dull. Generalisations about his work or thematic reductions look like disastrous box-office. *Antigone* is described as 'a collision between right and right'. *Oedipus Tyrannus* demonstrates 'man's powerlessness against Fate'. *Oedipus at Colonus* teaches 'acceptance beyond suffering'. Yet these are plays whose survival on a stage has been guaranteed less by their narcotic effect in tranquil reflection than by their capacity to raise the hair on the back of an audience's neck at a remove of two thousand five hundred years. The four plays in the present volume, *Ajax*, *Women of Trachis*, *Electra* and *Philoctetes* equally deserve their place in the modern theatre.

Aristophanes chose Aeschylus and Euripides as his dramatic adversaries in *Frogs*, but it does Sophocles no service to suggest that he represents a compromise between their two approaches. If that happens, then Aristophanes must take some of the blame by setting up his dramatic competition between a heavy-handed Aeschylus and a light-fingered Euripides, leaving Sophocles like some centre political party, with no support except from the uncommitted, but everybody's second choice. That does not reflect his authority as a playwright. In Sophocles there is no blandness.

He writes about pain and people in pain. A whole ninety years of watching pain and suffering pain feeds into his final play, *Oedipus at Colonus*, but the other six pieces that have survived from earlier in his career concentrate in due measure on emotional and physical suffering. That all the plays are exciting as well as agonising, and uplifting rather than depressing, suggests that here is a playwright whose experience of people and events, of personalities, catastrophes and the human capacity to endure them, has been honed by an instinct for true dramatic writing. Sophocles considers moral issues without moralising, offering through his plays aids to survival in a world whose most powerful forces are beyond individual influence or control.

The seven complete plays – there are some fragments and a substantial part of one satyr play in addition – amount to little over 10,000 lines, less than the three parts of Shakespeare's *Henry VI*. So meagre a portion makes the author hard enough to discover. The fact that there is a production date for only one of the seven, a provisional one for another, and that posthumous, and no more than speculation about the other five, makes any search for stylistic development 'like listening for a coherent answer among the oak groves of Dodona in a hurricane', as F. L. Lucas wrote about Nietzsche's views of Greek tragedy. But there are patterns and there are links.

What tends to happen to Sophocles' seven plays is that they get lumped into two baskets. Three plays deal with the story of Oedipus and his family and familiarly they are known as *The Theban Plays*. They were published as such in Don Taylor's translations in the companion volume to this in 1986. That they are likely to have been written, according to the more compelling arguments, over a thirty-five year span does not affect their unifying features: nor does Sophocles having started with *Antigone*, the last play of the saga, and then going on to write the two Oedipus plays which precede *Antigone*. All sorts of logic dictate that the three belong together. They are regularly presented so in revivals.

The corollary is that the remaining four plays also tend to get associated, as though they too possessed a unity of plot. To some extent there is such a unity, with the Trojan War providing the backdrop. The dying Heracles gave his bow to Philoctetes for agreeing to cremate him alive. Without that bow Troy could never fall. *Philoctetes* has here its link to *Women of Trachis* and, at the end of *Philoctetes*, it is Heracles who arrives *ex machina* to convince Philoctetes and Neoptolemos what they must do. At Troy, the death of Achilles, Neoptolemos' father, had led to his weapons being allocated to Odysseus and the subsequent shame and suicide of Ajax. Odysseus is a central figure in both *Ajax* and *Philoctetes*. In the former play, he resists his Commander-in-Chief Agamemnon in defending the right of Ajax to a decent burial. This is the Agamemnon whose murder on his return home at the hands of his wife Clytemnestra and her lover Aegisthus is avenged by Agamemnon's son Orestes in *Electra*.

This apparent continuity, however, conceals the fact that with each new play a Greek audience started again. The Heracles of *Women of Trachis* is not the Heracles of *Philoctetes*, the one a man, the other a god. And the crafty Odysseus of *Philoctetes* bears little resemblance, except in name, to the staunch defender of the honour of Ajax. Such versatility of character, as *Electra* shows particularly clearly, is one of the strengths of Greek tragedy.

There are more significant features of these four plays which identify them as the work of one man. Not least of these is that they could not possibly be mistaken for the work of Aeschylus or

Euripides. All revolve around a notion of dramatic effect and theatrical device which is uniquely Sophoclean. The great central figures, Ajax, Deianira, Heracles, Electra, Neoptolemos, Philoctetes, all live close to the edge. They face intolerable pressures, which some of them fail to survive. But whether we admire or fear them, these tortured creatures stand up on behalf of the human race. Aeschylus may overawe his audience at the way the gods function, Euripides appal them at how men and women behave. Sophocles deals in cause and effect, loss of honour that leads to suicide, love which provokes destruction, revenge within a family feud, the deceptions practised in the name of expediency. If the context is largely Homeric and the immediate reference a Trojan War long gone as far as the Athenians were concerned, never mind a twentieth-century audience, the characters still live as paradigms for strong emotions in crisis. Add to this what Don Taylor, in his Introduction to *The Theban Plays*, describes as 'a little bit of theatrical vulgarity', and you have a recipe that has lost none of its power over the years. The great playwrights – and there are not that many of them – do not date. From time to time they may go out of fashion. In a theatre which over the last twenty years has become increasingly confident in its means, it is exciting to watch the Athenian tragedians become a natural staple of the repertoire in new and inventive productions.

Ajax

Ajax is generally accepted as the earliest surviving play of Sophocles. It may be no more than coincidence but the earliest plays of all three Athenian tragedians are from late in their lives. Aeschylus had been producing plays for thirty years before *Persians* in 472 BC. Euripides was comfortably past forty when he presented *Alcestis* in 438 BC. There is no fixed date for *Ajax*. The mid-440s is a fair bet, but Sophocles was then already past fifty. It is the work of an experienced playwright and an experienced human being, a man who knew his audience, knew his theatre and knew his medium. What is there in the text is neither incidental nor accidental.

Ajax is not an easy play. It deals in moral paradoxes as well as moral problems. The Greek hero who gives the play its title manages to be both formidable and pathetic, but he is not easy to love. Pity and fear may have been emotions enough to satisfy Aristotle, but a modern audience tends to regard them as samples and ask for heroes who command respect and sympathy. If Ajax arouses such feelings, it is despite what he is, rather than because of it.

The suicide of the main character with so much of the play to run provides a structure less common today than in classical times. The effect is to throw a special emphasis onto the argument of the concluding scenes. The review of the dead by the living allows the audience too a time for reappraisal. The questions raised in *Ajax* during the burial debate between Agamemnon and Menelaus on the one side, Teucer and Odysseus on the other, have ramifications far beyond the immediate issue. What is a hero? What makes a friend or an enemy? What turns one into the other?

After the death of Achilles, the greatest fighter among the Greeks at Troy, there was a contest to see who should inherit his arms and armour. Though Ajax believed that Achilles would himself have bequeathed them to him, the commanders awarded them to Odysseus. Odysseus was known primarily for his cunning, a quality which proper heroes instinctively mistrust. A play like *Philoctetes* shows they have reason. So Ajax hates Odysseus and all the other Greeks, although he has been fighting on their side against the Trojans.

Sophocles' play opens when what Ajax has seen as his legitimate revenge for being slighted has been thwarted by the vigilance of the goddess Athena. Heracles appears as a *deus ex machina* at the end of *Philoctetes* but otherwise Athena's appearance is the only direct interference by god or goddess in a Sophocles play. She makes her appearance above the action – the human and the divine planes have their own stage space in Greek theatre – and is invisible to Odysseus. Having made Ajax mad so that he has killed and tortured animals instead of his enemies, she now invites Odysseus to enjoy the spectacle: 'What could be sweeter than the chance to laugh at him?' (79). Athena's code may seem savage but a Greek audience would not have found it unusual. What else would you feel for an enemy but hatred? But Odysseus replies:

> Yet I pity him
> although he is my enemy.
> This blindness could be set on me
> or anyone
> our lives are unsure
> flimsy things.

(121–26)

This is Odysseus' exit line. He is not seen again until he returns late in the play to argue that Ajax, though dead and disgraced, deserves the respect accorded to a hero. In his argument to Agamemnon Odysseus makes no mention of Athena's contribution to the saving of the Greeks from Ajax. It is as though her whole appearance has had only a figurative value for the rest of the story. What Odysseus does argue is that Ajax was a brave man – an enemy at the end, but a brave one – and that vindictiveness after his death 'will dishonour all the gods' (1343–44). This is not the impression you get from what Athena actually said. She was vindictive, thoroughly vindictive. Ajax had been arrogant and disrespectful, so for her addling his brains was quite a sport. In response to Odysseus' reflection on the flimsiness of life her retort was:

> Remember that then.
> Humble yourself before the Gods
> and sink your pride.
> Man's happiness is balanced
> on the knife's edge.
> Moderation is what we expect.
> We punish pride.
>
> (127–33)

Similar sentiments are echoed in any number of Greek tragedies. Pride, *hubris*, is the fault that most regularly leads to divine punishment. The knife's edge of happiness is a rather broader issue, with a human as well as a divine level. The speed of reversal of fortune is a natural part of the dramatic diet and Sophocles is not slow to exploit it, milk it even, in *Women of Trachis*, *Electra* and *Philoctetes*. In *Ajax*, and in the mouth of Athena, it acquires the force of a threat. Here she is saving Odysseus and his friends from being done to death by an arrogant bully and what thanks does she get? Odysseus, of all people, feeling sorry for Ajax. Let him take care.

Such provocation makes for one of the more forceful opening scenes in Greek tragedy, a scene which offers the clearest guidelines to the rest of the play. As a scene it suffers neither from the simplicity of the straight prologue, nor from the more mechanical devices of the standard exposition between two characters. Instead, it forces the audience bang into the middle of the main moral issues and suggests that solving the problems is likely to involve a revision of preconceived ideas. Those familiar with Brecht will find some apt parallels to Sophocles' dramatic method in *Ajax*.

Ajax himself is first seen as deranged, barely human, a Caliban let loose, fawningly grateful to the goddess for showing an interest in his vengeance. Little attempt is made at any time to conceal his vices. It is tempting as a result to downgrade his shame at discovering himself a laughing-stock, hated by gods and Greeks: downgrade it, not in the sense of denying its existence, denying rather that the experience is one which leads to a change in the man. But the nature of the man cannot be divorced forn the play's other issues.

When Ajax returns to sanity his thoughts are for his family. Speaking to the child Eurysaces he expresses hopes of revenge:

> your time will come
> > then
> > > show my enemies what sort of
> > > > man you are.

> (556–8)

He is concerned too for his aged parents and for his armour and certainly seems more humane than we have been led to expect. If he is meant to seem changed by his ordeal, then his two long speeches are likely to provide the key. In the first he convinces Tecmessa and the Chorus that he has accepted what has happened to him. In the second he prepares himself for his suicide. If he does go to his death unrepentant, 'horrifying as the obsessed are always horrifying', as R. P. Winnington-Ingram has suggested, then what are we to make of the respect that the Chorus maintain for him: or the love whch Tecmessa expresses and Teucer demonstrates in attempting to stand up to Agamemnon and Menelaus? An actor too may find himself drawn to an interpretation which makes the man the audience see more sympathetic than the monster the opening scenes lead them to expect.

The debate over whether or not the corpse shall be buried occupies most of the rest of the play after Tecmessa discovers the body. Teucer puts up with the scorn and insults of Agamemnon and Menelaus. He does not provide a convincing response to their argument. That is left to Odysseus who wins the day and gets permission for the burial by arguing for the respect due even to an enemy, for generosity of spirit and, with a disarming touch, for expediency. Who is to say whether the cunning Odysseus uses the fact that it may be in his interest to have Ajax properly buried as a cynical device, or as a clinching argument to someone who will appreciate a cynical device? Different actors, different productions. The rehabilitation of Ajax is dramatically flexible.

What can hardly be denied is that, villain or hero, Ajax suffers acute dishonour in a world where honour is important. His plight is emphasised first by the hostility of Athena, later, and more poignantly, in the staging of the suicide with the Chorus absent and the scene changed to the sea-shore. Such changes of scene are rare in Greek tragedy but have a theatrical purpose beyond the convenience of the plot. Here, the isolation of Ajax is given a physical reinforcement. Ajax confronts his death alone, accompanied only by a sword, not his own sword, nor Achilles' sword, to which he believed he was entitled, but a sword given to him by the Trojan leader Hector as a mark of battlefield respect from one hero to another. There are no living witnesses to his action.

If his previous behaviour has been taken as a challenge to the gods, all Ajax now asks of Zeus is to grant 'one small prayer' for his brother to find and protect his corpse. Ajax cannot forgive Agamemnon and Menelaus. But then neither does Odysseus forgive Ajax. What Odysseus argues for is a proper respect for what the man was. What he was – and that includes the element of extremism, of being not *sophron*, or 'sensible' – is precisely what made him a hero. Ajax remains unrepentant. He does not kill himself because he has had to face the fact that he is not a nice man. He kills himself because a goddess made him mad and because he performed, while mad, a series of actions for which he was not responsible. Sane again he cannot live 'without his name', as Arthur Miller's Eddie Carbone and John Proctor could not live without their names in *A View from the Bridge* and *The Crucible*. Normal rules are not appropriate for people like Ajax or the Heracles of *Women of Trachis*. Miller's heroes are ordinary people in extraordinary circumstances. Those of Sophocles belong in a world where superhuman tasks have to be performed. The sort of people who can perform such tasks become a liability when they are crossed. At the best of times they are difficult to live with. In *Women of Trachis* Sophocles turns his attention to the mightiest of all heroes, Heracles, and the issue takes on a new dimension.

Women of Trachis

Ajax is sometimes criticised as a broken-backed play because the hero dies with two fifths of the drama still to run. Three quarters of *Women of Trachis* is over before Heracles makes his appearance. By that time his wife Deianira has contrived his downfall, unwittingly, and committed suicide herself. She, rather than Heracles, could appear the central figure but Sophocles' title refers to neither of them. It refers to the Chorus. Their contribution to the plot is hardly significant but through them the relationship between the two main characters acquires its dramatic centre. *Women of Trachis* is not about Deianira or about Heracles. It is about Deianira and Heracles. The fact that they never meet during the action is a fair reflection of the life they have had together.

Heracles is one of the more flexible characters in Greek drama. He appears in six plays, two by Sophocles, two by Euripides and two by Aristophanes. Recognisable in Greek art from his club and lionskin, his given quality is sheer physical strength. Heracles was the strongest man who ever lived. He strangled snakes in his cradle and held the earth aloft when Atlas wanted a break. He dealt with all manner of monsters, as he points out in *Women of Trachis*, which threatened the various lands through which he travelled, or to which he was sent while doing penance for exercising his instinctive prowess and causing mayhem in the process. Beyond this strength the dramatists could, and did, turn him into anything from Samson to Desperate Dan, according to the mood of the piece.

In Aristophanes' *Birds* and *Frogs* Heracles is largely a figure of fun. Euripides introduces him initially into *Alcestis* as a dumb glutton who gets drunk and obnoxious until he discovers why the house of his host is in mourning. Once he is told that the king's wife Alcestis has died he sobers up fast enough and goes off to wrestle with Death. His other appearance in Euripides is in one of the most pathetic of plays, the *Madness of Heracles*. Arriving home after a long absence to discover his family about to be massacred, he saves the day, only to be struck down by madness, as is Ajax, inflicted by a hostile goddess. It is not sheep and cattle which Heracles slaughters but his own children. And in *Philoctetes* he makes an unexpected entrance at the end of the play to ensure that the main characters do the right thing.

Deianira in *Women of Trachis* describes her husband as 'the finest man who ever lived, whose like we'll never see' (812). Jane Austen would have been hard pressed to agree. '*Aristos*', the word Deianira uses to describe Heracles is not, however, a moral term. It is simply the superlative of 'good' and carries the implication of 'best at what he did'. To go with his enormous strength Heracles had enormous appetites, which Deianira recognises and accepts. 'Do you think there haven't been others?' she asks the startled Lichas, who has been trying to hide from her that the beautiful Iole is not just another prisoner, 'Other women in the life of a man like Heracles?' (459–60).

Everything Heracles does he does on the grand scale. There is little point in condemning him for moral flaws. That is Heracles and if you want a hero, don't expect him to be a great reader. Those who follow cricket will understand if I suggest that you put him in at number six and do not worry too much if his wickets are expensive. Heracles is a match-winner. Let non-cricketers look to the problems of entertaining an Alicibiades or a Coriolanus, an Ajax, if it comes to that, or any of those elementals with a special talent and whose exceptional qualities carry with them the seeds of self-destruction. Everything that Heracles does he does to the hilt. That includes suffering and it includes love.

In dealing with the power of love as a destructive force Sophocles is very much in the territory of the Euripides of *Medea* or *Hippolytus*, though both plays were written later than *Women of Trachis*. Medea, like Deianira, is a deserted wife who has recourse to a magic remedy. Medea knowingly destroys with a poisoned robe her husband's new wife before turning the knife on her own children. Phaedra, in love with Hippolytus, kills herself, leaving an accusation of rape against her innocent stepson.

By comparison with Medea or Phaedra, Deianira is an innocent in a world for which she was never made. She sends a tunic which she has anointed with a charm to her husband Heracles in the hope of winning back his affections from the young girl for whom he has just sacked an entire kingdom. Simple-minded, some might call her, as her magic potion is the blood of a creature killed when Heracles rescued her from the attentions of a randy centaur. How anyone could be so naive as to trust the centaur's dying advice that his blood will serve as a love-philtre if Heracles' eye begins to wander is an inevitable question. It seems to be the question which Sophocles sets up the play to answer.

Deianira is presented as someone in whom such gullibility is entirely plausible. She is a timid creature let loose in a savage world of grotesque monsters and sudden brutality. She is also, it has to be admitted, self-absorbed. An inordinate number of her sentences begin with 'I'. But there she is, a girl who has enjoyed a sheltered childhood and had the dire misfortune of turning out beautiful. Whether, in the ancient world, this was greater misfortune than turning out plain is a moot point. It does not do a lot for Deianira, on offer by her father as a bride for Achelous, whose triple aspect, described in her first speech, both creates the 'fear of sex' to which she refers and justifies it, when sex and marriage are associated only with savagery.

Saved by the intervention of Heracles, she learns to prefer fire to frying-pan, if only for the protection he can offer. That is quickly removed by his hardly ever being at home, and when he isn't at home she doesn't know where he is. When the play opens, her family have dispersed and she is living in a constant state of anxiety. All of this may account for her self-pity and her pessimism. Any cheery remark from the Chorus is met with a 'Yes, but . . .'. As it transpires, she has reason to be pessimistic. If her life before the play opens has been a sea of troubles, at least she has managed to keep her head above water. In 850 lines she goes under. Any exasperation she may initially inspire is surely dissipated by her kind reception of Iole, her dignity in the face of the insolence of Lichas and the hostility of her son Hyllus, and her pathetic attempts to remedy the situation in which she finds herself. The description of her suicide, when she discovers where her attempts to rekindle Heracles' love have led, is as poignant as any speech in Sophocles.

Deianira is what she is, just as Heracles is what he is. They are direct opposites. But what place is there in such a world for someone whose instincts are towards compassion? Euripides' Medea prepares the fatal robe to kill off Jason's new wife and proves that she is a more formidable force than anyone else in the play. Deianira makes a genuine mistake because she cannot treat Heracles' new wife except in a kindly way. She pays deeply for it. Hyllus may manage to persuade Heracles that Deianira did not intend to kill him, but Heracles' reaction is not to pity her or to blame himself. He wonders where she got the poison from.

To concentrate so much in a brief introduction on the interaction of characters may seem to emphasise a single aspect of the play at the expense of others. Aristotle points to *anagnorisis* and *peripeteia*, 'recognition' and 'reversal of expectation', as related dramatic features at which Sophocles excelled. They imply contrasts. *Women of Trachis* is full of both. They stem from the temperamental contrasts of the two central characters, Deianira, defenceless in a hard world, Heracles, the hard man, seen only when he can no longer stand up and complaining, in a way that borders on the comic, that not only was it a woman who laid him low, but that she didn't even have a sword with which to do it. Strength and weakness. Deianira is losing her beauty, Iole is young. Contrast and ambiguity, woven into the fabric of the play as cunningly as the contrast between sight and blindness is woven into the Oedipus plays. Oracles were celebrated in the ancient world for being open to misinterpretation. *Women of Trachis* is full of ambiguous oracles and omens. As Ajax needed to live out one day to find salvation, so Heracles faces a moment of crisis which will lead either to his death or to a long and tranquil life. Even the last oracle, which Heracles reveals on his deathbed, has the quality of a riddle:

> . . . no man alive would cause my death
> But some resident of Hell, a dead creature.
>
> (1160–61)

Heracles and Deianira may not be as bad as the Oedipus family for trying to avoid oracles, but it takes catastrophe for either of them to understand them.

The play proceeds, then, as do the others of Sophocles, according to this pattern of contrast in terms of theatrical as well as dramatic device. In this the tunic plays the main part, shown initially in a chest and under control. With heat turned upon it, this loving garment becomes a destructive force, eating into a man, even as strong a man as Heracles, and finally killing him. On his deathbed Heracles appears, still enveloped in the robe from which he cannot escape. The centaur gets his revenge but it is love which finally consumes Heracles. Heracles and Deianira may never meet during the play, but after her death her love remains in view, sticking to her husband. At the last, Heracles exacts a promise from Hyllus, a two-fold promise. Hyllus must see to his cremation. Philoctetes eventually performs this service for him. The second part of the promise is that Hyllus shall marry Iole. Heracles is still obsessed by love. Reluctantly, Hyllus agrees. Iole has no say in the matter, one need hardly add. Poor Iole, too beautiful and too gentle for such a world. Preserved from one man who has gone to war over her, she finds herself allocated to another. But, then, that was Deianira's fate too.

Electra

The story of Electra was well enough known when Sophocles presented his stage version. This is not another way of saying that the audience knew precisely what was going to happen on stage when they entered the Theatre of Dionysus to see *Electra*. Aeschylus had presented his version of the Electra story in the *Libation-Bearers*, the central part of the *Oresteia* trilogy, in 458 BC. Sophocles had probably attended that performance in the Theatre of Dionysus at Athens. It may have been as much as forty-five years later when he produced his own *Electra* but the story had not simply disappeared in between. After Aeschylus' death a special dispensation allowed for revival of his plays at the Great Dionysia, though Aeschylus, like other Athenian playwrights, had written in the expectation of a single performance.

Other dramatists before Sophocles, perhaps before Aeschylus, may have written of Electra, Orestes and Clytemnestra. Euripides wrote an *Electra* and an *Orestes*. The story of the house of Atreus was a source of reference in epic and lyric poetry, in art and in sculpture. Playwrights returned to familiar myth, not so that an audience could witness a story they already knew, but for the freedom such an outline could offer in creating a dramatic parable. As rehearsals for each festival production proceeded, no doubt word got round the small community of Athens about how any piece was shaping up. At the *proagon*, held a week before the festival proper, the competing playwrights and their casts each gave a public trailer of their production. These did not include close detail of the treatment, which was still a novelty for the audience on the day of performance. The presence of Clytemnestra and Orestes in the cast-list of an *Electra* would guarantee that son killed mother rather than the other way round. But, as in all the world's greatest plays, the dramatic impact arose less out of what was done than how it was done. The Electra of Sophocles is dramatically exciting because she is not the Electra of Aeschylus or the Electra of Euripides.

Fortunately for scholar and critic all three Electra plays have survived, but they have not survived solely as texts for study. The *Oresteia* and the two *Electra*'s deserve and receive regular stage revival. What these revivals demonstrate is not the similarities between Aeschylus, Sophocles and Euripides, but their differences. Giraudoux, Sartre and O'Neill have shown in our own century that the characters are far from exhausted. The value of myth resides in its flexibility within parameters.

Sophocles' *Electra* may or may not have preceded Euripides' play. Opinions differ. What is not in doubt is that both playwrights must have known their *Oresteia* and known that their versions would be to some extent judged against an acknowledged classic. Euripides takes the bull by the horns and sends up the Aeschylus recognition scene between Electra and Orestes, using a ferocious black humour to demolish the plausibility of the tokens by which Aeschylus' Orestes reveals himself to his sister. Euripides may have been responding to Sophocles too in a reading of the story which demolishes any sense of heroism and reduces the murders to a level of dumb brutality.

Sophocles appears to challenge Aeschylus' basic moral and criminal paradox. A son must avenge a murdered father, according to the Homeric code. Where is his duty if the murderer is his mother? Aeschylus investigates the impasses and out of it creates the model for a new concept of justice, one that is in accord with the rising power of Athenian democracy. Sophocles' Clytemnestra is a monstrous creature but revenge is centred on Orestes and Aegisthus, leaving Eiectra at the play's heart. To suggest that Sophocles ignores the question of matricide, and is therefore uninterested in it, is too simple. It is a matter of moral focus and Sophocles' emphasis is less on the action than on the character of the heroine. In his first speech Orestes declares that he has consulted the oracle at Delphi about avenging the murder of Agamemnon. Apollo's reply was:

> Go yourself, helped by no army.
> Use tricks to snatch the punishment.
> They killed; they must die.

(34–6)

This stark statement brooks no argument. Nor does it get any. Orestes, Pylades and the Servant plan the revenge like a military exercise. The deaths of Clytemnestra and Aegisthus are to be executions. The cases have already been judged, the moral decisions made. The audience never see Orestes meet Clytemnestra. Any sense that the death of his mother may provoke the Furies against Orestes, as in Aeschylus, or feelings of repugnance and despair or an attack of conscience, as in Euripides' *Electra* and *Orestes*, is ruled out when Orestes returns moments after the killing with the words:

> It is all right. Inside, it is all right,
> If Apollo's prophecy is kept.

> (1425–6)

A couple of lines later, Orestes and Electra are preparing for the real climax of the revenge, the murder of Aegisthus. The order of these two killings, Clytemnestra's followed by that of Aegisthus, is the single most pointed difference between Sophocles' version and that of the other two playwrights. Taking the heat off the issue of matricide may be part of the intention, but it also clears the way for one of Sophocles' bits of 'theatrical vulgarity'. The body under the sheet, which Aegisthus believes to be Orestes but is actually his wife, offers a touch of the macabre familiar in drama of the Renaissance but rare in the Greeks. The gratuitous theatricality, gratuitous in the sense that Orestes could have stage-managed the whole operation with far less risk, does have the dual effect of grabbing the audience and distracting them from asking any of the more awkward questions that the previous ten minutes may have raised. Revenge is revenge.

This is an Homeric world, not an Athenian one. The story of what happened to Agamemnon at the hands of Aegisthus and Clytemnestra is related in the *Odyssey*. Orestes' actions are there held up as the perfect model of filial behaviour for Odysseus' son to follow. What Sophocles does is bypass the question of justice raised by Aeschylus and return to Homer. His *Electra* is thereby a revenge drama, but at the same time a moral play of which even Plato might have approved: Oscar Wilde's Miss Prism too, for whom the 'meaning of fiction' was that 'the good ended happily and the bad unhappily'. In *Electra* the good appear to end happily and the bad dead.

If this was all there was to the play, it would seem not much more than *Deathwish 400 BC*. Sophocles centres the play dramatically, not on the revenge of Orestes, but on Electra herself, who makes virtually no contribution to the planning or execution of the plot. The playwright sets up a meeting between brother and sister in the opening scene but then arranges that they do not meet until line 1099 or become reunited until line 1222 – four fifths of the way through the play. Everything in the intervening period concerns Electra. Once she has made her entrance she never leaves the stage. She shares her grief with the Chorus, argues with her sister Chrysothemis, confronts her mother Clytemnestra, listens to the Servant's long description of her brother's supposed death in a chariot-race and overwhelms Chrysothemis' optimism at finding the offerings at Agamemnon's tomb. In all of this the audience may feel sympathy, but in an oblique way. The first scene has ensured that they are aware that Orestes really has returned. All Electra's wretchedness is based on mis-information. The effect is to pin-spot her character, expose it like a specimen on a slide.

Any concern over her future is tempered by prior knowledge that the plot is getting on quite happily without her. Without this concern over what will happen to her, we can look instead at what has happened to her. Almost despite the plot, the play is about Electra. The other characters pale into insignificance beside her. They seem like cyphers, adopting whatever roles they feel appropriate, but without the resources to carry them through. Only Clytemnestra can in any way match her, recognising her as a true daughter and, therefore, a threat to be put away. The play is practically a monodrama.

What has kept Electra going is a hatred as powerful as the humiliation of Ajax or the physical pain of Heracles and Philoctetes. She has fed on her hate, absorbing humiliation almost with relish. As the play progresses, so her passion is revealed as having dimensions. She may scorn her sister's pragmatism, but she knows how to use her. The reported death of her brother leads her beyond despair to attempting vengeance in person. The strength of her character is never more clearly shown than when Orestes finally faces her but without her realising who he is. As with the destructive tunic in *Women of Trachis* Sophocles again uses a theatrical device to concentrate the emotion of the scene. The urn which Orestes brings, pretending that it contains his own ashes, passes into Electra's hands and acquires a stage life of its own. So much does her response affect Orestes that he breaks his resolve to remain incognito. The delayed recognition offers a dramatic enough reversal. The transformation of Electra's misery into passion for her brother borders on the perverse as she at last finds proper fuel for her desire for revenge.

It must at least cross the mind of an audience, as it will of an actress, to wonder what will remain when her excuse for living has been removed. Euripides creates an Electra who has made a profession out of misery and whose mind appears to have snapped with nothing left to feed on. Sophocles' heroine is made of sterner stuff, but passion of this order doesn't melt away. Her passion will need some outlet. No other character in Sophocles is so central nor so single-minded, not Antigone, not Ajax, not Philoctetes, not Oedipus. The play is hers and hers alone. Electra is the finest female role, perhaps the finest role, in Greek tragedy.

Philoctetes

In his *Classical Dictionary* published at the end of the eighteenth century John Lemprière claimed that Sophocles surpassed Euripides in 'the sublime and the majestic'. That was a period when Greek tragedy was seldom seen on a stage. The plays survived in the study or the classroom. An audience encountering *Philoctetes* today may wonder about the sublimity of infected rags lying in the sun to dry or the majesty of a malodorous foot. The sheer physicality of the play and the realism of its detail seem more Euripidean than Sophoclean.

Philoctetes was a member of the Greek army which set out against Troy. When he trespassed at the shrine of Chryse he was bitten on the foot by a snake. The wound festered and the combination of the stench and his groans led the rest of the Greeks to abandon him on Lemnos. When the play opens he has been living there for ten years like Ben Gunn in *Treasure Island*, with the wound getting worse rather than better, able to survive only because he possesses the bow of Heracles and arrows which cannot miss their mark. Now the Greeks need the bow.

This bow provides a link through to Sophocles' earlier *Women of Trachis*. In that play Heracles, another hero consumed by pain, tries to get his son Hyllus to end his father's torment by burning him alive. Hyllus agrees only to make the preparations and so *Women of Trachis* ends. According to the myth it was Philoctetes, son of the King of Trachis but no great hero in his own right, who lit the pyre. In gratitude Heracles bequeathed him his bow and he was allowed to keep it when the Greeks marooned him. After ten years they have discovered that the capture of Troy depends on the bow and Odysseus and Achilles' son, Neoptolemos, have come to fetch Philoctetes.

On the face of it, such a quest sounds the stuff of an adventure story but hardly of a tragedy. Yet all the three Greek tragedians wrote a *Philoctetes*. Only the Sophocles version survives, but there is an essay by Dio Chrysostom, written during the first century AD, in which he compares the Philoctetes plays of Aeschylus, Sophocles and Euripides. Euripides is the playwright usually associated with realism – Aristophanes ridiculed him for dressing his kings in rags – but it does seem that on this subject it was Sophocles, not Euripides, who made the feature of Philoctetes' physical degradation, the bandages, the stumbling walk, the agonised spasms and cries of pain.

The part of Philoctetes requires great physical as well as emotional range, making demands on the actor, as the present translator has noted, far in excess of those required for Ajax or Oedipus. There is an additional difficulty, beyond the ordeal for the actor, of showing agony on stage. An audience can easily reach the point of saturation past which sympathy is no longer engaged. Sophocles is taking a major risk, it seems, in what he is asking his actor to do.

What saves the play is that the pain which has warped Philoctetes' life comes to represent one side in a competition with Odysseus for the soul of the young Neoptolemos.

Aeschylus would appear not to have included Neoptolemos as a character in his *Philoctetes*. Euripides certainly omitted him. Perhaps, before Sophocles, he had had no part in the story. Here, he provides the whole moral focus. Son of the dead hero Achilles, Neoptolemos is one of Sophocles' innocents. Odysseus has brought him along to help trick Philoctetes because the young man is both plausible and biddable. Neoptolemos soon finds himself the battleground between two implacable foes. In his presence each reveals himself, but it is Neoptolemos who begins to change, growing in stature as he finds the strength to resist Odysseus and make his own decisions.

Odysseus is the same character as appears in *Ajax*. There his arguments are honourable and lead to the burial of a man who has been his enemy. In *Philoctetes* he demonstrates more of the glib tongue and craftiness commonly associated with him. Not that he makes any bones about what he wants of Neoptolemos:

> You must cheat Philoctetes,
> And tangle his soul in a net of words.
>
> (54–5)

He is to ingratiate himself by pretending to have fallen out with the Greeks, Odysseus especially:

> Call me any names you like.
> Spare me no insults. He must believe you,
> Or else you bring ruin on all the Greeks.
>
> (65–7)

The arguments are forceful and pragmatic, a politician's arguments, perhaps a soldier's, but in his love of intrigue Odysseus miscalculates the calibre of the people he is trying to manipulate. As the inheritor of the arms of Neoptolemos' father Achilles, Odysseus ought really to be a match for one cripple, even a well-armed one. He prefers to rely not on the weapons of Achilles, but on the son of Achilles and the pretence that he is upset by losing his father's inheritance.

Odysseus cannot resist pretence. He cannot resist doing things by stealth. His first entrance has him barely venturing into view while directing Neoptolemos to establish contact. His next intervention is not in person, but by proxy, sending a servant disguised as a trader who embroiders the story so unnecessarily that some critics have thought it must be Odysseus under the disguise. Odysseus next appears in person in mid-line, at precisely the moment when Neoptolemos seems to be wavering in his loyalty. It is almost comic, as though he had been lurking in the wings for the last eight hundred lines, like a stage-manager checking that everyone is sticking to the script. As the end will show, there is such a stage-manager, but it is not Odysseus, who is simply revealed as someone who enjoys intrigue for intrigue's sake and justifies himself to Philoctetes with the words:

> I'll say just this:
> I make myself the man each occasion demands.
> When honesty and justice are required,
> I am the justest, most honest man alive.
>
> (1048–51)

Deep down in Sophocles there is a fascination with the roles people play and the masks they adopt. Each of the plays in this volume has at least one major scene which hinges dramatically on a complex process of deception. Perhaps it is what attracted him to the theatre.

Odysseus returns twice more in the play, first in pursuit of Neoptolemos who has decided to return the bow to Philoctetes. His last entrance is hardly an entrance at all, as he is so busy trying to keep out of Philoctetes' range that he may even call his lines from off-stage. On this occasion Neoptolemos has to save Odysseus from the angry Philoctetes. So much coming and going adds constant new twists to the plot. At each turn the relationship between Philoctetes and Neoptolemos develops up to the point at which they decide to forget Troy, defy the Greeks and head for home. That is when the real stage-manager intervenes, Heracles, who arrives as a god, *ex machina*, to convince the two of them that they cannot fly in the face of the future. They must go to Troy.

The arrival of a god to re-establish the myth is a device associated more with Euripides than Sophocles. *Philoctetes* is a late play, produced in either 409 or 408 BC. Perhaps Sophocles was consciously adopting a method perfected by his rival. The artificiality of the device draws attention to how the original myth has been hijacked by the stage characters, Pirandello-fashion, so that the problems become living issues rather than twists in a fabulous tale. Neoptolemos' change of side makes a plea for compassion, a plea for decency in a devious world. The intervention of Heracles can point to that while still suggesting that always, and particularly in time of war, there is likely to be conflict between public duty and private conscience.

Whatever emerges as the central issue, and in each production that may be different, the play will always hinge on the dominating figure of Philoctetes, from whom Sophocles never allows too much distraction. His own physicality is given extra weight by the symbolic status of the bow. As *Woman of Trachis* makes use of the tunic and *Electra* the urn to round out the suffering of the protagonist by the power invested in a property, so the bow has its own stage life. It fires arrows which never miss. Helenus, the prophet from Troy, has revealed that the city will never fall until the Greeks possess it. Control of the bow provides the play's major dramatic and theatrical rhythm. Odysseus' wary entrances are dictated by its being for him an object of fear. When Neoptolemus has it Odysseus can relax and be himself. The bow creates situations and levels of human relationships. For Philoctetes it is more.

Philoctetes is one of the stage's great solitaries. R. P. Winnington-Ingram has made the point that, as a result of his confinement, Philoctetes has peopled the island of Lemnos with objects, the cliffs, his cave, domestic paraphernalia. He personifies the pain in his foot. The bow has made survival alone possible. It is his gift from Heracles and his only friend.

Sophocles' heroes and heroines possess an aloofness which makes them treat people like things, as well as things like people. Antigone demands the privilege of acting alone. Creon ends that way. Oedipus prides himself on his superiority. Ajax removes himself from the company of human beings to the company of Hector's sword and an empty stage. Deianira's loneliness extends to never again meeting Heracles, himself unique. Electra stands apart, unaware of, and at a tangent to, the drama unfolding round her. Philoctetes discovers that the state to which his foot has condemned him may be redeemable and rejects the offered cure.

Such is probably the quality of heroes. Hamlet, Brand, and, dare one say it, Mother Courage, acquire their strength in the same kind of way. Perhaps this is where Sophocles' 'sublimity and majesty' resided for Lemprière. Aeschylus' heroes reveal their humanity in rare flashes, Euripides' are too human to be heroic. Sophocles creates special cases, men and women exceptional for what they do, what is expected of them and what happens to them. For those today who are unwilling to pay heed to the exceptional individual, Sophocles' plays may seem remote. So may Athenian democracy and a society that was chock-a-block with exceptional individuals. The more open-minded will find that the issues and arguments of these plays are no more confined to the deep past than are those of Shakespeare, Ibsen or Brecht.

The line-numbering alongside the texts relates to the Greek original rather than the English translation.

J. Michael Walton
University of Hull, 1989

Transliteration from Greek into English presents problems of consistency. The names of the playwrights are more familiar as Aeschylus, Sophocles and Menander than as Aischulos, Sophokles and Menandros. Otherwise direct transliteration has normally been adopted while allowing for previous translations in the series.

AJAX

Translated by Robert Cannon

Characters

AJAX, a warrior
TEUCER, his half-brother, son of a war-slave mother
TECMESSA, Ajax's slave-wife
EURYSACES, Ajax's son by Tecmessa
ODYSSEUS, a warrior
AGAMEMNON, leader of the Greeks
MENELAUS, his brother
ATHENA, the Goddess
CHORUS OF AJAX'S SOLDIERS

Before the tent of AJAX *in the Greek camp outside Troy.*

Enter ATHENA *above, then* ODYSSEUS.

ATHENA.
Odysseus
      always on your enemy's track
      looking for a way to catch him
now I find you on the camp's edge
      hunting Ajax down
      out by the ships
sniffing
   like a blood-hound.
      Is he here or isn't he?
He's just arrived
   sweating heavily and blood-stained   10
so
   stop looking and   come out with it
what are you after?
Ask me anything you like.

ODYSSEUS.
Athena
   first of all the Gods to me
   invisible
      but still a living presence.
Your words strike at my ear like
   trumpet calls –
Yes
 I'm after Ajax
      with his mighty shield.
 But not revenge this time
   I've come to find out what he's up to   20
   what he really tried to do
      to all of us
      last night.
All we know for certain is
 our sheep and cattle
      and their guards
      were butchered
         savagely

3

and Ajax is suspected.
Someone saw him running
        with his sword still dripping
        with fresh blood.
30   I've followed him but I can't understand
        the foot-prints.
        Your arrival is well timed.

ATHENA.
I know.
        I felt you needed me
and came to help your hunting.

ODYSSEUS.
Am I on the right track?

ATHENA.
Yes   Ajax is the man . . .

ODYSSEUS.
40   Why did he do it?

ATHENA.
Because he failed to win Achilles' armour.

ODYSSEUS.
Why attack the cattle?

ATHENA.
He thought that he was killing you.

ODYSSEUS.
The whole Command?

ATHENA.
Yes   and he was nearly
able to.

ODYSSEUS.
How did he think he'd
get away with it?

ATHENA.
I baulked him
as he crept up in the dark.

ODYSSEUS.
  How far did he get?

ATHENA.
  To the generals' tents.

ODYSSEUS.
  How did you stop him?   50

ATHENA.
  I turned his brain with
      thoughts of wild revenge
    and in his ecstasy he fell upon the cattle
            and their keepers
     all the loot you'd kept for
     sharing round
    carved out a slaughter-house
    piling carcasses around him.
  Agamemnon, Menelaus no one
     escaped his sword
    as he cut deeper into the trap I'd set.   60
  Finally he dragged the few
     he'd missed
                back
    prisoners
   into his tent where he is torturing them.
  I'll show you –
    so that you can tell the rest
      what he has done.
  Don't cower there
    he won't recognise you.   70
  Ajax!
  Leave your prisoners and
  Come outside!

ODYSSEUS.
  What are you doing?

ATHENA.
  Silence   you're not frightened?

ODYSSEUS.
  No   but leave him be.

ATHENA.
  What scares you?
    He's a man.

ODYSSEUS.
  And deadly enemy.

ATHENA.
  Then what could be sweeter
    than the chance to laugh at him?

ODYSSEUS.
80   I'll laugh at him in there.

ATHENA.
  You're frightened of him!

ODYSSEUS.
  Only because he's mad.
  If he were sane I'd face him.

ATHENA.
  And you still can.
    He won't see you.

ODYSSEUS.
  Why?

ATHENA.
  Because I've warped his sight.

ODYSSEUS.
  The power of the Gods!

ATHENA.
  Stay still then.

ODYSSEUS.
  If I must.

ATHENA.
  Ajax
90   is this the way you treat your friends?

  Enter AJAX.

AJAX.
  Hail Athena!

Welcome
    child of Zeus!
    Come   let me dress you
    with my spoils of war.

ATHENA.
  Indeed you may but
        tell me –
  is your sword well soaked in
        Greek blood?

AJAX.
  Certainly it is.

ATHENA.
  Your generals' blood?

AJAX.
  They won't sneer at me again.

ATHENA.
  You've killed them both?

AJAX.
  I have   and now I'll keep my armour.   100

ATHENA.
  What happened to Odysseus after all?
    Did he escape or
    have you   dealt with him?

AJAX.
  That double dealer.

ATHENA.
  Your worst enemy.

AJAX.
  He's in there
        my prize captive.
    He won't die   too quickly.

ATHENA.
  What will you do with him?

AJAX.
First   tie him to the tent pole

ATHENA.
Poor wretch   and then?

AJAX.
110   Flog him till he bleeds
            then kill him.

ATHENA.
Must you torture him like that?

AJAX.
I'll do anything you ask –
    except to change my plans for Odysseus.

ATHENA.
Well if you feel so strongly
    do as you want.

AJAX.
I've work then   pardon me.
But I'm grateful for your interest –
       believe me   Lady.

Exit AJAX.

ATHENA.
That is a God's power Odysseus.
Who was wiser, abler or
      more thoughtful than this
120   Ajax?

ODYSSEUS.
No one.
Yet I pity him
  although he is my enemy.
 This blindness
    could be set on me
        or anyone
our lives are unsure
      flimsy things.

Exit ODYSSEUS.

ATHENA.
>   Remember that then.
>   Humble yourself before the Gods
>> and sink your pride.   130
>   Man's happiness is balanced
>> on the knife's edge.
>>   Moderation is what we expect.
>>> We punish pride.

Exit ATHENA. Enter the CHORUS of AJAX's soldiers.

CHORUS.
>   Ajax
>   Prince of Salamis
>>   I rejoice when
>>> you are fortunate.
>   But when the Gods
>>   or men
>>   reject you
>   I recoil.   140

>   Out of the dark
>>   a wind of rumour blows.
>   Did you stride into the night
>   trampling the grass
>   wielding and wasting with your sword?

>   Odysseus feeds us
>>   with these stories
>   and we listen to him –   150
>   so many drunk with pleasure
>>> at your downfall.

>   A great target is fair game
>>   for anyone.
>>   Envy seizes on the rich and fortunate
>   and
>>   a high tower needs   160
>>   foundations of great stones
>>   with rubble swept between.
>   Yet
>>   the vulgar never learn this lesson.

You my lord
  are our protection from
      corrosive ignorance.
  Show yourself
  fall on them with your talons
170   strike and rend them
        blathering.
        Silence them.

Is Artemis to blame for these wild rumours?
    Did you forget to honour her?
Is some dark God using you to
180   undermine the army's unity?

Only madness
    could have driven you to do these things
        if you have done them.
But
    if the generals and
    Odysseus   curse him
if
    they have believed it and accused you –
Oh my lord
190   we beg you   save yourself
          we beg you   leave your tent
                        and save yourself and
          save our name.
Show yourself   Lord Ajax
reassure us.
    I am full of sorrow but
    your enemies are mocking you
200   and glorying in your shame.

Enter TECMESSA.

TECMESSA.
  Ajax is overwhelmed with
      troubles.
  Those of us who followed him from Greece
      and honour him
      share in his sorrow.

CHORUS.
  What has harmed him
        Tecmessa?   210
  What has happened?
    He loves you and he must have
        told you what it is.

TECMESSA.
  The words stick in my throat
        but you'll hear it
        all too clearly
        all too soon.
  Great Ajax is possessed
  his tent   awash with blood
    like an unholy altar.   220

CHORUS.
  So it is true then
    everything they say about him.
  What next   what more?
  Our leader will be put to death
        disgraced!   230

TECMESSA.
  Some of them have had their
    heads sliced cleanly off
  others have been hacked to pieces.
  There were two white rams
        he chose especially –
    one has had its tongue cut out   240
    the other is still tied to the tent pole
        he flayed it with his whip
        and cursed it as he flogged it
            mercilessly
  like a frenzied God   and not a man.

CHORUS.
  A man with any sense   250
    would leave   now
                      hide
                      slip out or
                      cast-off quietly.

Both the generals
　　Menelaus and Agamemnon
　will be here   and I dread to think
　　　what we may have to share
　　　　with our master.
I pray his fate will not be ours.

TECMESSA.

He is calm now   sitting
　　buried in the heap of his own wretchedness
　as he gazes on his handiwork
260　　tortured by the slow awakening.

CHORUS.

Surely anything is better than
　　the fit he suffered.

TECMESSA.

But unaware
we suffered for him
now
　he suffers also
doubly.

CHORUS.

With us and because of us.

TECMESSA.

He is cured and we are all
　left full of pain.

CHORUS.

270   What do you mean?

TECMESSA.

He was joyful in proportion to his lunacy
　　　although we weep for him.
Now he is sane again
　a vice of misery and anguish grips him.
He was better off before.

CHORUS.

I understand.
But it is natural.

Some God has planned this.   280

TECMESSA.
  It must be.

CHORUS.
  But
    tell us truthfully what happened?
    We are all in this together.

TECMESSA.
  In the middle of the night
    all the campfires out
  Ajax armed himself and stood
      by the tent flap.
    I tried to ask him
    what he was doing – who
    had called him, summoned him? –   290
  'All the army is asleep'.
  He only quoted
      'Silence is a woman's virtue'
  and went out.

  I don't know what he did then
    but he came back with a
    mass of animals
    and set about them
    mutilating   beating   killing them
    and cursing them like men
  while they stared at him hopelessly.   300

  At one point he cried out
      dementedly
    that he had paid Odysseus, Agamemnon
        and the rest
        back.

  Then he slowly started
      to calm down
      and realise what he had done.
  He sat there   in the blood
    a beast among the beasts he'd butchered.   310
    Tore his hair out.

Eventually he asked me
   on the pain of death
  to tell him what had happened.
I was terrified
  and said what I had seen
  and then he cried a cry
320   such as I have never heard
  such as he despised in others
   when he used to stifle
    his own anguish.

It is over and he's lying in there
eating nothing   drinking nothing
  fallen with the carcasses.
But he's planning something –
  that is why I came to find you.
  Won't you come and try to comfort him?
330   You are his friends.

CHORUS.
How terrible this is.

AJAX.
God help me!

TECMESSA.
Worse may follow.
Listen!

AJAX.
Oh my God!

CHORUS.
Either he's mad again
  or horrified at what his madness did to him.

AJAX.
Where is my son?

TECMESSA.
340 He wants Eurysaces   why?
I don't know where he is   what shall I do?

AJAX.
  Where is my brother?

CHORUS.
  Open the tent   perhaps
      he'll calm himself if he sees
          us.

TECMESSA.
  There –
      judge for yourselves

  Enter AJAX.

AJAX.
  Now friends
      still faithful to me   350
      look at this flood-tide of misery!

CHORUS.
  Tecmessa
      it is true.
  A dreadful madness.

AJAX.
  Friends
      strong oarsmen
      hardy seamen
  help me in my agony   360
          and give me death.

CHORUS.
  Don't say that.
      Don't ask for cures worse
          than the illness.

AJAX.
  Look at me!
      Mighty warrior!
          Ajax!
  Conqueror of sheep and cattle.
  Look at my shame.

TECMESSA.
> My lord I beg you
>> do not think of that.

AJAX.
> Out of my sight!
370 > Oh God!

CHORUS.
> My lord   control yourself.

AJAX.
> How could I have
>> let my enemies escape
> and murder animals instead?
>> What curse took hold of me?

CHORUS.
> Forget what you have done.
> You cannot alter it.

AJAX.
> Oh yes
380 >> Odysseus
> sneaking through the camp
> with your slanders and your mischief
>> what a victory this is for you!

CHORUS.
> Laugh or weep
> just as the Gods demand.

AJAX.
> Show him to me.
>> Even so!

CHORUS.
> My lord
> you are in no position
>> to even think like that.

AJAX.
> Zeus
>> our family's great

                                                    390
    ancestor –
  help me kill them
    and then die my own death.

TECMESSA.
  If that is what you want
    then pray for my life too.
  You are my life.

AJAX.
  The sun throws shadows over me.
    I am in the blackness.
    I can only live now
        in the dead world –
    I have damned myself.
  No God or man will help me   400
  I am Athena's broken toy.

  Where shall I run to?
    Where can I hide?
  I have lost myself.

  I have died with these pathetic
        creatures.
    Friends help me
  the whole army is about
    to march against me.

TECMESSA.
  Listen to him –
    he is utterly destroyed.   410

AJAX.
  Troy
    your beaches and your battle-fields
      won't see me anymore.
    and the mountain-tops
    and rivers that   420
      we fought for
        listen now –
  this is the last of me.
            Let me be proud
            once more:

the greatest warrior of all the Greeks
will never march out over you
again.

CHORUS.
I cannot bear to hear this
but I know I must.

AJAX.
430   Ajax – Agony
has my own name damned me?
There is no else to use the word
this is my Agony.
My father fought here
and won honour
hero among heroes.
I came to Troy
and fought here also
a great champion of my people
fought among the heroes.
Yet I was rejected
and my crown is infamy.
440   But I know for certain that
Achilles
would have nominated me
to have his armour.
Who else was worthy?
But our generals
have robbed me of it,
gave it to a worthless
to a scheming nothing of a man.
I can tell you
450   If Athena had not blinded me
Agamemnon and his brother
would have never cheated anyone again.
I was set to strike them
ready to be at them
when she turned my mind
and they escaped me
in the blood of these dumb animals.
Instead   I am their laughing stock.

The Gods grant victory just
  as the fancy takes them.
Now
  they're set against me
  and the Greeks revile me
  and the ground I stand upon rejects me.
  How can I stay here?
  How can I sail home   460
    and face my father?
    Empty handed
    and no victory crown!
Should I try to find
  some final glory
    hurling myself alone against
      the Trojans
    gain a victory for Agamemnon?
There must be some other way   470
    to prove myself
  bring back   honour for my father
  not spin out a waste of time
    with dreams and hopes
      or hopes of nothing
        a long easy nothing
          endless   pointless
            cheap enough.
    To die with honour!
    There is
      nothing else.
That is all there is.   480

CHORUS.
  There is no point lying.
  You have opened up
    your secrets to us
  but still
      let us try to reason with you.

TECMESSA.
  My Lord
      the hardest thing of all
    is learning to accept our fate.

I was a king's daughter
490   and I am your slave.
        You were the Gods' instrument
      but now there is no man I love or
                 honour more than you.
Don't waste us
   let me pass on
      to another's bed
        be mocked at.
Don't leave me
      and your son
       to be
   dragged off to be some other Greek's
500   slave
   constantly reminded of my
        happiness with you
and ridiculed for my new wretchedness.
'Look – she belonged to Ajax
   champion of the Greeks.
How are the mighty fallen!' But
It will be you and all your family
      not me
       they'll mock.

Your father and your mother pray for you
       wait anxiously for your return.
     Don't leave them to a childless old age.
510   Don't rob your little son of any hope
       left to foster-parents and neglect.
You destroyed my country
   killed my father and my mother
sent them down to Hades   Now
     if you desert me
       what is left?
Don't steal my .everything I have from me
      my lord and father
        shield
520   my life.
You owe me something   surely.
What shall I have to think if you

      repay
    all those who love you
    with such empty kindness?

CHORUS.
  Ajax is there
    no pity in your heart?
    Won't you consider what she says?

AJAX.
  Yes I will consider it
    if she obeys me   now.

TECMESSA.
  Ask lord. Only ask.

AJAX.
  Bring my child here.   530

TECMESSA.
  I hid him for his own sake.

AJAX.
  Explain yourself.

TECMESSA.
  You might have killed him.
        in your blindness.

AJAX.
  That would have pleased
        some God or other!

TECMESSA.
  I took care of him.

AJAX.
  And you were right.
  Now bring him here.

TECMESSA.
  The servants have gone looking for him.

AJAX.
  Where is he then?

TECMESSA.
Eurysaces
            your father's waiting.
      Bring him quickly.

AJAX.
540   Where is he?

      EURYSACES *is brought in.*

TECMESSA.
   Here.

AJAX.
   Give him to me   put him in my arms
      don't worry –
   if he's my true son the blood
            won't frighten him.
   He's got to become used to it
   to follow me
550   be like his father.
   Boy   be as I have been
         in everything save luck
   and you'll be a complete man.
   I envy you your innocence
         free of pain
         happy in your ignorance
            the greatest happiness.
   Live your springtime to the full
      nothing too much
      not pain   not joy
   your time will come
      then
         show my enemies what sort of
                     man you are
               your father's son.
   Until then   be a child
   and make your mother happy.
560   No one here will harm you
               in my absence.
         Teucer my close friend and brother

even if he's off in battle
will protect   watch over you.
And my countrymen
I charge you as you love me
report this to him
tell him to take my son home
so that he may care for
Telamon
my father
and my mother
Eriboia   570
in their old age.
My armour shall not be left as a prize
for any of the Greeks.
This shield
my son
whose name I gave you
will be yours
my great shield
packed with seven sheets of ox-hide
yours to hold and fight with.
All the rest I'll keep
in my grave.
That's all.
Now
take the child away
close my tent up
and be silent.
No women's wailing.   580
The surgeon doesn't weep or tremble when he
holds the knife.

CHORUS.
I am afraid for you
Lord Ajax
Too hasty and too sharp.

TECMESSA.
What will you do my Lord?

AJAX.
Don't question me!

TECMESSA.
By the Gods
    and for your child's sake –
    don't abandon us.

AJAX.
Enough of that.
I owe the Gods
590   nothing.

TECMESSA.
Be careful!

AJAX.
What care did they take?

TECMESSA.
I beg you
    think again.

AJAX.
Enough.
That is enough.

TECMESSA.
I am afraid my lord.

AJAX.
            Now
            shut me in.

TECMESSA.
Relent
    and change your mind.

AJAX.
You know me
    and you ask me that?

Exit AJAX. EURYSACES *is taken out.*

CHORUS.
I remember our own country

island Salamis
in the sea spray   600
        peaceful
loved by all the Greeks.

I have grown old
exiled in a tent here
    far away from you
and hopes of seeing you again
    begin to fade.

Death's terrifying land
    seems closer to me now.

Now I have to sit here
    vainly nursing Ajax'   610
        sick soul.
A shadow of the man who brought us here.

Salamis
        you sent him out here
        as a warrior among warriors.
Full of blackness   620
    now
his sword-hand
desperately wrings his shield-hand
    and the brothers Agamemnon, Menelaus
    have forgotten all his victories
        and plot revenge.
We watch him
    full of pity.
There is nothing else that anyone can do.

What will his mother do
    when she learns of his tragedy?
Can her old body
    hold the grief she'll feel   630
    or will it burst her heart?

He would be better
        dead.
    He isn't Ajax
            any more

only a mad shadow of himself.
640 What will his father do
when he hears of it
hears what curse fell
on this great son of his
house?

Enter AJAX.

AJAX.
Time shows up everything
and swallows it again.
There is nothing that a man
can know for sure.
Anything is possible.
Iron bent and shattered
after all.
I was sharp and mettled as this sword
650 and now a woman's words
have softened me
with pity for her and my child
an orphan and a widow
left alone.
I am going to the sea's edge
I shall wash and purge myself
and pray Athena's anger
has been satisfied.
I'll bury my great sword
deep in the earth
lose it to myself and
660 all mankind.
Hades keep it.
Since dead Hector gave it to me
it has brought me nothing
but disaster.
Neither honour nor respect
and it's true   an enemy
gives nothing with his gift.
I'll learn to serve the Gods
and serve our generals.
The law is theirs and we have to

    acknowledge it.   670
All the harshness of the world
is overcome   eventually.
Winter melted into Spring
the Night flies at the Sun's warm
        thrust.
The storm subsides
  the sea left calm
and Sleep is forced to let us
        slip into the day's first light.
I accept the Gods' will.
I shall honour Agamemnon as my
           rightful master.
I have learnt this –
  hate an enemy knowing he may be my friend   680
  love a friend knowing he may be my enemy.
  Men are tricky things.

Go in and pray for me   Tecmessa.
Pray the Gods may grant me
  what I ask.
  You too my friends.
Ask Teucer to take care of me and mine
      and all of you.
I am going where I have to   690
  where my peace waits for me.

    Exeunt AJAX *and* TECMESSA.

CHORUS.
  Now is a time for dancing.
  Cross the seas
    Pan!
  Over mountain snow tops
    Come Pan!
  Lead us as you
    lead the Gods' dance   700
  teach me to be joyful
  teach me your wild dances
    God Pan!
    And Apollo

follow him
across the sea too
fly
teach us your music
your bright singing.

The Gods have wiped my tears away.
Dawn's brightness
710   lifts the veil and
        Zeus
we see your world again.
Ajax' pain is over
  he is brought to know
    the Gods' strength
  makes his will their will.
Time is everything
  he has made peace in his soul
    with all the world.

Enter MESSENGER.

MESSENGER.
Friends   Teucer
720   Ajax' brother has come back.
Before he even reached the camp
a crowd of soldiers started
    harassing him
    shouting   taunting
    threatening and spitting at him
  calling him the brother of a madman and a traitor.
'Cut him down   make sure
    he doesn't get away
let's stone him – '.
730   Drawn swords and bloodshed
    but one of the old men stopped them.
Where is Ajax now?
I have to speak to him.

CHORUS.
He has changed his mind   and gone
to make peace with
    his destiny.

MESSENGER.
  God help him then!
  I've come too late.

CHORUS.
  Why?   740

MESSENGER.
  Teucer insisted that he must
      stay here until he came.

CHORUS.
  But he's gone
          to purify himself clean
              before the Gods.

MESSENGER.
  If Calchas' words were right
      it was a foolish thing to do.

CHORUS.
  What words? What
      do you mean?

MESSENGER.
  Only what I say.
  When Calchas left the Council tent
  he parted from the generals   750
      and went to speak to Teucer
      grasped his hand and
  urged him
          do his utmost
          to keep Ajax in his tent
          keep him out of sight
          just for this one day
  if he wanted him to live.
      Athena's anger would be spent
          by nightfall.
  The Gods hate pride
      man puffed up with his own achievements   760
          ready to be slapped down   ripe

for calamity.
From the start it seems that
Ajax has ignored this.
His father had advised him to pray
for victory with the Gods' blessing
but he boasted that anyone could conquer
like that
he intended making his own glory
770   by himself.
Athena came once   standing by him
in the battle
told him what to do   again
he replied in words
no mortal tongue should speak
and told the Goddess to protect
those who needed her   he could
hold the line alone.

This man thought himself an equal of
the Gods
and Athena hated him.
If he lasts today out   then he may
survive
780   with the Gods' help!
That was Calchas' message.
Teucer sent me here immediately
to tell him.
But too late.

CHORUS.
Tecmessa
come out and add this to your
stock of misery.

Enter TECMESSA.

TECMESSA.
I have only just recovered from one blow.
What now?

CHORUS.
Listen to the messenger.
I can only weep.   790

TECMESSA.
    What is it?

MESSENGER.
    If Ajax has indeed left
            fear the worst.

TECMESSA.
    He has.
        Explain yourself.

MESSENGER.
    Teucer has sent word
        that Ajax must not leave his tent
                alone.

TECMESSA.
    Where is Teucer?

MESSENGER.
    He's only just arrived back at the camp.

TECMESSA.
    Why did he order this?   800

MESSENGER.
    Calchas the prophet warned him
        that today would either kill
                or save his brother.

TECMESSA.
    Friends
            help us!
    Some of you run to fetch Teucer
    all the rest   spread out along the beach.
    You comb the eastern side
        and you the west.
        I'll go as well   810
            all   search out Ajax.
    Now I understand what he was saying.
    Come

>   quickly
> there is no time to lose
>   if we want to save his life.

CHORUS.
>   We are ready
>   to do everything we can.

Exeunt CHORUS, TECMESSA *and* MESSENGER.

The Seashore

Enter AJAX *with the sword*

AJAX.
>   Strong   sharp   and deadly
>   as you should be
>   final enemy
>   Hector's gift
>   wait there   patient   ready
>   on this Troy ground that detests me

820
>   whose stones have whetted you
>   prepared
>   a last good friend
>   to give me death.
>   I have done as much as I can do
>   now
>   Zeus   one small prayer –
>   let my brother be the first
>   to hear of this
>   the first to lift me up
>   my body
>   when I am dead.
>   Don't let an enemy find my corpse

830
>   and spread it out for birds and dogs
>   to mangle.
>   Hermes   take me into the dead world
>   with one sharp thrust
>   no lingering.
>   Furies   greedy audience
>   at Man's tragedy

watching for revenge
note how Agamenon and Menelaus
have destroyed
and mark them down for ruin.   840
As they forced my hand
against myself
so let the hands that owe them love
strike them both down
and more   revenge me on
the whole Greek camp
destroy them   utterly.
Apollo   hold your burning chariot still
for just a moment
over Salamis and let my
father and my mother understand
what has been done here.
Oh mother
what a cry will rend our city and
how useless   all of this.   850
Enough.
Now only Death.
Strong Hades   Lord of Death
stand by me   I
attend you shortly in your kingdom.
For the last time   light
the God Apollo
Sun God
Light!
and glorious Athens
Troy   your plains and rivers
comrades
wife and child
brother and
the sun
the day
my country
Salamis   my home!   860
I greet you with the last words
I shall speak
among the living.

AJAX *falls on his sword*

Enter CHORUS 1.

CHORUS 1.
  Look   search   keep on
  looking.
  There   and there too
870   is there anywhere we haven't looked?
  We have covered the whole beach
  to this side   surely.
  Who's there?

    Enter CHORUS 2.

CHORUS 2.
  Friends.

CHORUS 1.
  Well?

CHORUS 2.
  We've covered every inch
  of seashore to the west and found

CHORUS 1.
  What?

CHORUS 2.
  Nothing?

CHORUS 1.
  Nothing this way either.
  Not a trace.
880   A fisherman late
  spreading nets out on the sands tonight
  a spirit from Olympus
    or a sea nymph
  one of these perhaps
  will find him
  wandering about and tell us.

CHORUS 2.
  Pray God one will
  we've covered the entire bay and

haven't found
a footprint or a sign of any kind.   890

   Enter TECMESSA.

TECMESSA.
  No! No!

CHORUS.
  What's that. From over there.

TECMESSA.
  God help me now!

CHORUS.
  Tecmessa!
  Look.
  Our lady. Look at her.

TECMESSA.
  I am lost!
  Now everything is taken from us.

CHORUS.
  Why? What?

TECMESSA.
  Ajax   still warm   blood wet
    body scabbarding his sword.

CHORUS.
  Our only hope is gone.   900
  My lord
    I die with you
  my heart breaks
    for your deserted wife.

TECMESSA.
  He is dead
    and I have only my own tears
       to comfort me.

CHORUS.
  Who did this to him?

TECMESSA.
He did   look
his hand is
910   still gripped on the hilt.

CHORUS.
My blindness and
my deaf stupidity
my carelessness
are all to blame.
Show me
my unlucky master –
Ajax
caught up in the agony of his own name.

TECMESSA.
You cannot look.
His body must be shrouded in this robe.
What friend of his
could bear to see the sword
stuck
deep inside him   and the life blood
920   crusted on his lips?
Who can help me?
Who will carry him?
Where is Teucer?
No one else can do it
fetch his brother's body
wash it
give it proper burial.
Ajax   so great and so completely
ruined
even your enemies must weep for you.

CHORUS.
I can see
that nothing could divert you
from your fated path
930   down to destruction.
The hatred that you felt
the anguish in your soul and voice

could only lead to this.
I knew it all as soon as I had heard you
        cry out against Agamemnon and his brother.
All this was branded on your heart
  when you failed to win
Achilles' fatal armour!

TECMESSA.
  I cannot bear this!

CHORUS.
  Her heart will break.
  We understand your agony.

TECMESSA.
  Unbearable.

CHORUS.
  Such loss   so suddenly.   940
  We understand.

TECMESSA.
  I know you do
    but the pain is still all mine.
  My little son
    what slavery will he share with me
                    now?

CHORUS.
  God forbid that
    Agamemnon or Menelaus
  should force that on you.

TECMESSA.
  Yet it would be the Gods' will too.   950

CHORUS.
  Too much   They ask too much of us.

TECMESSA.
  This is Athena's work
    all done to please her favourite
  Odysseus.

CHORUS.
Time-serving
    evil-hearted man
waiting for our troubles
        entertaining
960   Agamemnon with them.

TECMESSA.
Let them laugh.
    They wanted to be rid of him
now he is dead
    they'll soon wish he was
    fighting for them
    when the pressure's on.
Fools only know what they once had
    when they have lost it.
His death brings them less pleasure
    than me sorrow
    and him
        satisfaction.
He wanted it   a death that suited him
    and it is something now between him
970   and the Gods.
Let them say what they want.
    Ajax cannot hear them
he has gone   and only
    left this misery behind.

TEUCER.
God help me!

CHORUS.
Teucer! Look.

    Enter TEUCER

TEUCER.
Brother   Ajax!
    Is it true?

CHORUS.
Yes.
He is dead.

TEUCER.
    The loss is terrible.   980

CHORUS.
  And therefore

TEUCER.
      Oh terrible   too terrible!

CHORUS.
  We must mourn him and

TEUCER.
        I cannot bear to think of it.

CHORUS.
  Weep for him Teucer.

TEUCER.
      And more.
  Where is the little one?

CHORUS.
  By the tents.

TEUCER.
  Go back immediately and fetch him
    they may take him
    as they steal the lion's cub after its mother
        has been killed.
  The world takes quick advantage
    of the dead.

    Exit TECMESSA

CHORUS.
  His last wish
    was that you'd care for Eurysaces.   990

TEUCER.
  Nothing I have seen
    is as dreadful as this sight.
  No road I've ever trod
    has had so terrible an ending
      as the one I took

to learn what had become of you
>> my brother
>> best beloved.

My soul groaned when I heard the news
spread through the camp
> that you were dead.

Now I am here

1000 the sight itself becomes a living death.

Come let me see the worst.

Uncover him.

Dear God!

Hatred and unbending resolution
> ground into your face.

What kind of life have you left me?

Who will hold a hand out
>> to a brother who so failed to save his brother?

What will Telamon our father say?

1010 What will he look when I return? A man
> who never smiled in happy hours!

Call me a war-slave's bastard
> coward in your time of need
> a traitor to our family

or worse
> believing that I left you to your death
> to take your place when you were gone!

Deaf to reason   any argument
> that's how he'll brand me
> in his bitter rage.

I shall be exiled   robbed of all my rights

1020 >> and freedoms

That is the home you've left me.

And meanwhile
> in Troy

I shall immediately inherit
> your enemies.

These are the gifts and future
> that you leave me with.

And that great sword
>> still bright
>> sliced through you

We shall strain to drag you up
        off it
  your executioner   so
 Hector slew you finally
  dead Hector
  and your destiny.
Just think of it
  the ironies of time and fate –
Ajax gave great Hector a fine girdle   1030
  and it dragged him from his chariot
  pulled behind the horses
  till it killed him.
Hector gave Ajax a fine sword
  and it killed him too.

The Furies or the God of death
  forged both these things.
Whatever anyone may say
I know
    that destiny
 is a net the Gods have woven for us.
If you think otherwise
   so be it   I know
  what I know.

CHORUS.
 Teucer   this is a time for action.   1040
  Quickly think of how to bury him.
  Someone is coming
      an enemy no doubt
   to laugh at Ajax' ruin.

TEUCER.
 Who is it?

CHORUS.
 Menelaus   the man who got us all
  to come here in the first place.

TEUCER.
 Yes   Now I recognise him.

   Enter MENELAUS.

MENELAUS.
  Wait!
  Leave that corpse alone.
  Don't touch it.

TEUCER.
  On what authority?

MENELAUS.
1050   My own and the High Command's.

TEUCER.
  For what reason?

MENELAUS.
  I'll tell you.
    We brought Ajax here
    as a friend and ally.
  We have found him a worse enemy
        than any Trojan.
  He planned to kill us all
    by stealth by night.
  Only the Gods' benevolence has saved us
        otherwise
    it would be him standing over
1060   our dead bodies.
  Instead his sword was turned on mere
        brute animals.
    Thank the Gods –
  He will have no rites of burial.
  He will lie out on the sand
        and feed the gulls.
    No argument –
  we had enough of that when he was
        still alive.
  We could not rule him then
1070   but now what we command will be obeyed.
  He never listened to superiors
    and no army town or state
  survives without
    obedience and respect for rank.
    Without it

the law has no force in the state
the army has no discipline.
None of us is greater than
    our destiny.
At the height of power
    remember   accident.
Fear and shame are the bedrock of society   1080
  individual self-will destroys it.
A strong law
  not individual caprice
    I say.
Respect and order.
Don't believe that we can
    put the payment off forever.
Pride before every fall   he had his turn
                now it is mine.
Leave the corpse alone
  or start to think about a grave
        for yourself.   1090

CHORUS.
  Menelaus   your principles are good.
    Don't compromise them by
        offending against the dead.

TEUCER.
  How can an ordinary man
    be expected to be virtuous
  when the high born talk like that?
  You brought him here?
  He came at your command?   he sailed
    with his own ships as his own master?   1100
  Whoever gave you power over him?
  What right have you to order his own people
              now?
  You came as king of Sparta   at what point
    did you become our general?
  He owed us just the same as you owed him
    no more no less.
  You sailed out on the same conditions
    as the rest of us.

You and your brother
                    rule your own subjects
                        punish them!
    I shall bury Ajax as the dead
1110   must be buried
        despite you both.
    He didn't come here to fetch back your
                    wretched wife
                        like some paid servant
        he had sworn an oath   that's all   and kept it.
    He had no interest
            in you or what you thought.
    You can come and tell me what to do
        and your brother and your heralds
        but I don't pay attention
                        to the likes of you.

CHORUS.
    Be careful Teucer
        you are in no position
            however justified
        to talk to him like that.
    You'll cut yourself.

MENELAUS.
1120   This bowman has a high opinion of himself!

TEUCER.
    I'm not ashamed of my war skills.

MENELAUS.
    How would he sound if he were a real swordsman!

TEUCER.
    I'm more than a match for you
                just as I stand!

MENELAUS.
    A fierce tongue   sir!

TEUCER.
                Right entitles me to it.

MENELAUS.
    And your brother had the right
            to kill us all?

TEUCER.
Kill you all? You look alive enough to me!

MENELAUS.
Only by the Gods' protection.

TEUCER.
Then be grateful to the Gods
and leave their work alone.

MENELAUS.
I   meddle with the Gods?   1130

TEUCER.
Yes
if you forbid
this burial.

MENELAUS.
Allow my enemy a
proper funeral?

TEUCER.
When did he ever challenge you?

MENELAUS.
We loathed each other
and you know we did.

TEUCER.
For good reason.
You cheated him
of Achilles' armour.

MENELAUS.
Blame the judges
not me.

TEUCER.
Clever
and two-faced.

MENELAUS.
You'll pay for that.

TEUCER.

> Whoever gave the real offence
> will pay.

MENELAUS.

For now just understand one thing –
1140 No burial.

TEUCER.

> You understand.
> He will be buried.
> Now!

MENELAUS.

I once saw a braggart   just like you
  persuading men to take a boat out in a storm.
When the storm got up
    he hid himself
      and the sailors treated him as he deserved.
You sound loud enough now
    wait for the storm to break
1150   and then watch out.

TEUCER.

I once saw a pompous fool
  insulting neighbours when their luck was down.
One of them
    warned him
    to outrage the dead
    at his own peril.
The advice was well-meant
    but a waste of breath.
Do you follow me?

MENELAUS.

I don't need to stand here
  arguing with you   what
  do you take me for?
An army's waiting for
1160 my orders.

TEUCER.

And I'm afraid they'll laugh at me

for listening to your braying!

Exit MENELAUS.

CHORUS.
Teucer
　　brace yourself
　　for a fight.
Quickly
　　make the grave   shallow   anywhere.
He must not be forgotten.

Enter TECMESSA *with* EURYSACES.

TEUCER.
Here are his wife and son
　　in time to honour him with proper rites.

Come child   1170
　　kneel beside the body of the one
　　　　who gave you life.
　　　now hold him and receive these
　　　　locks of hair   mine

　　　　　　　　　yours
　　　　　　　　　your mother's
　　　tokens of our eternal union
　　　binding us together in his name.
If anyone tries to
　　force you from the body
　let his corpse lie unburied
　let him be utterly cut off from
　　　　　　his own race
　　　as these locks are cut off
　　　　　from our own bodies and our kinship.
Now
　hold him boy
and keep watch over him.   1180
Friends
　　　don't hang back like frightened women
　　help him keep his watch while I'm away
　　　　　preparing Ajax' grave
　　　　　whatever anyone may say.

Exit TEUCER.

CHORUS.
> When will I have earned my final rest?
> When will all my years be counted out?
>   I long for that. Each day of them
>   marched out in front of Troy
> is choked with battle-dust and shame
>   for all the Greeks.

> Whoever first revealed the arts of war
>   be damned.
> He should have died first.
> All the generations of man are his
>   slaves.

> He wrenched me away
>   from peace and friendship
>   spilled my wine cup
>   broke my flute
>   my night's rest
>   and my loving.

> Who cares about me
>   living in the mud and dirt
>   alone
>   now
> of this Trojan waste?

> Lord Ajax cared for us
>   and shielded us.
> Now fate has stolen him
>   and spilt his
>   life blood on its altar.
> We have lost our only comfort.
> This wretched empty sand.
>   Think of the pine woods
>   and a bright sea lapping by them.
>   Athens   what wouldn't
>   any of us give
>   to see you now?

Enter TEUCER.

1190

1200

1210

1220

TEUCER.
  I had to turn back
    Agamemnon's coming.
  Wait and hear his venom!

AGAMEMNON.
  You
    are the fool
  who's been shouting off his mouth about me?
  And been allowed to get away with it?
  You
    slave-woman's son
      trying to protect a corpse
      denying my authority.
    Questioning our High Command
      our right to order anyone.
    Claiming Ajax came out independently.
  Slave-woman's son!
  If you'd been free born
    nobly born   God help us   1230
    what would you have said then?
  Ajax
    what about him?
  What did he do
      that I didn't?
  Was he the only warrior we had?   1240
  Achilles' armour
    isn't that it?
    Damn it, and my decision for awarding it!
    I gave it up to open ballot.
  But a slave here
    Teucer
  won't accept the way the voting went
  and I've got to listen to his lies and slanders
  and accept this Ajax' right to murder us
          because he didn't get his way.
  But I'm not having it
    the law has got to be upheld
    if we are to survive at all.
  Enough. A strong man can't be allowed

to flout the law
because he threatens us.
1250 We're not interested in a man's brute strength.
A very small whip is enough to guide an ox
along the road.
I hope you understand me.
Ajax is a corpse now
and a corpse
can't save its friends.
Remember who you are
and control your tongue.
If you want me to listen
1260 get a free man to speak for you.
I won't listen to your babblings any more.

CHORUS.
Be reasonable
both of you.
For all our sakes.

TEUCER.
How easily men forget what
they owe the dead
and then betray them.
This man has not one single
thought for you   Ajax
1270 although you risked your life for him.
Everything forgotten in the emptiness.
Remember now –
when Hector charged the camp
and set fire to the boats
and you
were trapped behind the lines
who saved you?
Single-handed saved you and your men
from a disaster?
Ajax the man you've just
belittled in your pride
and still you ask 'What did he do I didn't?
1280 Was he the only warrior that we had?'
Who leapt at the chance when

his name was picked out
drew his ballot and
rejoiced that he was chosen
as the champion to fight with Hector?
Ajax did these things
and I
a slave's son
stood by him.
You ignorantly taunt me with my birth.   1290
Pelops your grandfather was a barbarian.
Atreus your father made his brother eat
his own son's flesh.
Your mother was an adulteress
caught with a foreign slave in bed
and drowned for it by her own parents.
You taunt me with my birth:
My father was a hero
Telamon
my mother was a Princess   1300
chosen for him by great Heracles
a fitting prize for what a hero'd done.
Both my parents were of royal blood.
My only shame would be
if I failed to maintain my brother's honour
failed to help his wife and child
all of which your orders desecrate.
Understand this –
if you dishonour Ajax
and cast his body out
you will have to kill us and pile up
our corpses heaped on his.   1310
I would rather die for him than for your wife
or is it Menelaus' wife?
Think of your own position therefore
or you may regret
what you have done.
Better give way and be called a coward
than risk such uncertainty.

Enter ODYSSEUS.

CHORUS.
> Odysseus   if you are here to help
>   rather than stir things up
>   your cunning was never more welcome.

ODYSSEUS.
> I heard raised voices
>   some way off.
> what is going on here?

AGAMEMNON.
> This fellow
1320 >   has been speaking his mind
>   my lord Odysseus.

ODYSSEUS.
> What did he say? He may
>   have been quite justified.

AGAMEMNON.
> I cautioned him when he
>   insulted and defied me.

ODYSSEUS.
> What did he say to so offend you?

AGAMEMNON.
> He ignored my orders
>   and swore to honour Ajax' corpse.

ODYSSEUS.
> Agamemnon   will you take offence
>   at a friend's well-meant advice?

AGAMEMNON.
> If I were a fool.
1330 >   Speak.
>   You are my closest ally.

ODYSSEUS.
> Then listen.
> Don't let hatred or blind rage
>   destroy the law.
> Remember you too are a man

and let the corpse be buried.
Don't let personal revenge
    mislead you.
Since I won Achilles' armour
                Ajax
  was my enemy as well
  my deadliest enemy of all.
                  Nevertheless
        I can't dishonour him in death
  or deny his bravery.
We both know that Achilles
      among both the Trojans and the Greeks
      alone surpassed him.   1340
If you disgrace him now you will
      dishonour all the Gods.
He was your enemy but it is beneath
    contempt to seek revenge upon a corpse.

AGAMEMNON.
  Are you on his side
        my lord?

ODYSSEUS.
  I am
      although I hated him
      as long as hate was justified.

AGAMEMNON.
  And now he's dead
      stamp on his corpse.

ODYSSEUS.
  A meaningless   unthinkable triumph.

AGAMEMNON.
  Kings cannot afford such niceties.   1350

ODYSSEUS.
  Nor to discount good friendship and advice.

AGAMEMNON.
  I was his king and general.

ODYSSEUS.
> To know when we are wrong
> is to win a great victory.

AGAMEMNON.
> Think who you are honouring.

ODYSSEUS.
> A noble enemy.

AGAMEMNON.
> Who you are helping.

ODYSSEUS.
> My respect is worth more to me
> than my hate.

AGAMEMNON.
> A curious change of attitude.

ODYSSEUS.
> A wise man always keeps an open mind.
> Men change.

AGAMEMNON.
> As Ajax changed
1360   into an enemy.

ODYSSEUS.
> Mere stubborness is not a sign of strength.

AGAMEMNON.
> If I back down
> it will look like cowardice.

ODYSSEUS.
> Generosity   my lord.

AGAMEMNON.
> You want me to permit the burial?

ODYSSEUS.
> In the end it is a right
> each of us claims.

AGAMEMNON.
So
your concern is really for yourself?

ODYSSEUS.
What else?

AGAMEMNON.
Let this be known as your work then
not mine.

ODYSSEUS.
It doesn't matter.
You will be judged
in the right.

AGAMEMNON.
You are my friend and I am happy   1370
to grant any request.
Do as you want
now.
But for myself
I can only hate
the man.

Exit AGAMEMNON.

CHORUS.
Only a fool would still
misunderstand your subtlety
Odysseus!

ODYSSEUS.
Teucer
let me be your friend
as much as I have been your brother's enemy.

I beg you to allow me
to join in honouring
and burying your brother.
Pay last respects to the great dead.   1380

TEUCER.
Words fail me.

        I have
deeply wronged you.
You hated him most of all the Greeks
    and only you defended him.
Agamemnon and Menelaus ordered his body
        to be left to rot
        unburied and dishonoured.

1390   I pray that Zeus may strike them both
        that Justice and the Furies
           may pursue them
and that they may suffer
    the same fate that they asked
        for him.

And yet
    as I respect and honour you
Odysseus   forgive me –
    I cannot ask you
        to attend the corpse.
    But you may take part in any other
        of the funeral rites
and so may any other Greek you wish to bring.
Believe me
    your name will be engraved on all our hearts.

ODYSSEUS.
1390 I understand
    although I wished to help you.
I respect your customs.

TEUCER.
  Quickly now
    begin the preparations.
Some of you dig the grave
others   start to wash
    the corpse
      fetch wood and kindling
        set the cauldron on the fire
the rest
    bring his great suit of armour
        out.

Boy
  use all your child's strength   1410
      to help lift your father's body
              gently.
For all your weakness
                  he will feel your love.
Dead   yet his life blood warms his flesh.
Come
  all the friends of Ajax
  help bear him up.
He was one of the noblest
and most perfect warriors in Greece.

CHORUS.
  We can understand what we have seen.
  We know nothing of our future
  Our lives are lived out
    in the face of mysteries.

WOMEN OF TRACHIS

Translated by J. Michael Walton

Characters

DEIANIRA, wife of Heracles
NURSE
HYLLUS, Heracles' and Deianira's son
MESSENGER
LICHAS, Heracles' herald
AN OLD MAN
CHORUS OF LOCAL WOMEN OF TRACHIS
IOLE (non-speaking)
WOMEN CAPTIVES (non-speaking)

Before the house of HERACLES, *in Trachis.*

Enter DEIANIRA, *wife of* HERACLES, *and a* NURSE.

DEIANIRA.
It's a long-established saying amongst men
That no one knows his fate before his death,
Nor how his life will turn out, good or ill.
Well, I know mine. It will not take my dying
To recognise my life as ill-starred, full of grief.
When I was still in my father Oeneus' house
I first acquired a desperate fear of sex,
Worse than any unmarried girl in Aetolia.
It was a river asked father for my hand,
I mean, of course, Achelous, who had three forms.   10
First he would come as a raging bull and then
In the shape of a wriggling snake, or else
In the form of a beef-faced man with a sooty beard
Spewing out water like a river in spate.
With the threat of a lover like that confronting me
I prayed for death to release me once and for all
From the horrors of this monster's marriage-bed.
And, in the nick of time, to my relief,
The son of Alcmena and Zeus came to the rescue,
Great Heracles, who made a formal challenge   20
To try and set me free. What kind of battle they fought
I can't say. I didn't see it. If you want to know
You'll have to find someone who dared to watch.
I cowered there, paralysed with fear,
The fear that beauty like mine can only lead to misery.
Zeus decreed that the fight should end happily.
Happily, I suppose. But since I've been Heracles' wife
I've worried about him ceaselessly, night and day.
Fear breeds fear. Night follows lonely night,
Dispelling some fears, creating others, worse.   30
We've had a family but he sees them no more often
Than a farmer visits his boundary field,
Once to sow it, and then again to reap it.
He's hardly set foot in the house and he's off again.
That's his life, always at someone's beck and call.

But now he's finally completed all his labours
I'm even more frightened than I was before.
Since he killed the powerful Iphitus,
I've stayed here in Trachis, living on charity,
40   In a stranger's house, an exile from my home.
Where he's taken himself off to, who can say?
I'm here without him, left to suffer alone.
I can't help feeling something terrible's happened.
It seems an age since he went away this time,
Ten months now and more, add another five to that,
And not a word from him. Yes, something terrible.
He left behind an oracle when he went. Here's its message.
I hope and pray my anxiety's unfounded.

NURSE.

Deianira, my mistress, many's the time
50   I've seen your face all tear-stained just like now,
Sorrowing for your absent husband, Heracles.
If you'll accept the right of a slave to advise
Someone freeborn, listen to what I have to say.
You're not short of sons.
Why not send one of them to go and find him?
Hyllus would be my choice, if he's prepared to do it.
He'd soon find out how his father fares abroad.
I can see him now, hurrying towards the house.
If you are prepared to follow my advice,
60   This would be a good moment to tackle him.

DEIANIRA.

Hyllus, my son, please wait. Sometimes the lowborn
Can give us good advice. This woman here
Has given me 'free' counsel, though she's a slave.

HYLLUS.

Really? You'd better tell me, mother, what I'm to hear.

DEIANIRA.

She pointed out that you've never once inquired
Where your father is and she finds that wrong, she says.

HYLLUS.

I know where he is, or where they say he is.

DEIANIRA.
    If you know, Hyllus, why don't you tell me?

HYLLUS.
    He spent last season, at least, this is what I heard,
    Serving some Lydian woman as her slave.   70

DEIANIRA.
    If he could sink to that, anything's possible.

HYLLUS.
    I've also heard that he's freed himself of her.

DEIANIRA.
    And do your sources suggest he's alive or dead?

HYLLUS.
    They say he's making war, or he's about to,
    Against the city of Eurytus on Euboea.

DEIANIRA.
    He left behind an oracle, did you know that too,
    With some prophecy that relates to Euboea?

HYLLUS.
    I know nothing about that. What does it say?

DEIANIRA.
    It says that he will either end his life
    Or, if he can complete one final labour,   80
    He'll find peace and live to a serene old age.
    I'm sure his fate lies in the balance as we speak.
    Please, Hyllus, will you go and help him, if you can?
    I don't know how we'd survive your father's death.
    For better or worse our fate is tied to his.

HYLLUS.
    Of course I'll go. If you hadn't kept these prophecies
    So close, mother, I'd not have stayed till now.
    He's always been a lucky man in the past, you know.
    I saw no reason for your being so concerned.   90
    But now I do understand and will not spare
    Myself in finding out the truth, the whole truth.

DEIANIRA.
> Do go, Hyllus, go now. However late it comes,
> Once we hear it, good news is always welcome.

Exit HYLLUS. *Enter* CHORUS.

CHORUS.
> Sun-God, oh Sun,
> To whom starry night gives birth as she dies
> And at twilight kills you in turn,
> Tell me, I beg, please tell me,
> Where may I find Alcmena's noble son?
> Sun-God, oh Sun,
100 Whose shining eye brings everything to light,
> Do the twin continents hold him fast?
> Where is he? Is he there still?
> Or driven through the sea-straits restlessly?

> Deianira,
> Like a bird which dare not face its fate,
> Piteous, her mind awash with tears,
> With eyes that can weep no more.
> Poor battle-prize, Deianira.
> Deianira
110 Feeds on fears for her roaming husband,
> Lonely, ever hoping fearfully,
> Ever fearing what she hopes,
> Like a widow, Deianira.

> The winds of heaven
> Swirl and storm, South and North,
> Toing and froing, restless as the waves.
> So struggles Heracles,
> Always against the odds,
> Fighting the currents of his laboured life.
120 And yet, there is a God,
> Some guardian God, it seems,
> Who keeps him from Death's premature embrace.

> So I can chide you,
> Lady, though with respect.
> Why do you choose to disregard your faith?

The Lord of Heaven decrees,
Despite your suffering now,
That no one's life be wholly free from pain.
As the Great Bear revolves
Across the starry heavens,   130
The scale of good and evil balances.

And as the darkest night
Will always yield to day,
In poverty or wealth,
In happiness or grief,
'This too will pass'
Is always true for men.
So you must never court despair,
But ask yourself, as I do now,
When did Zeus ever abandon one of his sons?   140

DEIANIRA.
I suppose you must have heard of my distress
And that's why you've come. I hope you never face
The depths of anguish into which I am sinking.
The young grow up cherished in their own home,
Protected like hothouse plants from too much heat or shade,
And neither storm nor gale will trouble them.
A girl can live a sheltered life and be quite happy.
But marriage changes that.
A woman now, she faces nightmare fears
For her husband, and, if not for him, for her children.   150
Unless you're married yourself you can't
Understand how weighed down I feel with anxiety.
I've put up with so much already,
But nothing to compare with this. Let me tell you.
When Heracles went away on this last occasion,
He left behind a tablet with an inscription.
The tablet was old, one I'd seen before,
But he would never tell me what the writing meant,
However daunting his enterprise. He always left
Like a hero, not someone facing death.   160
This time was different. He read me his will,
Disposing of his effects as though he were a dead man,
Something for me and a share of his land for each child.

He set a fixed time, one year and a further three months.
When that had passed, from the moment he left the house,
Then he must face death. But if he proved able to survive
This crisis, all would be well and he could expect
To live his life out in tranquillity and peace.
The Gods themselves had decreed it, so he told me.
170   Heracles' troubles were to be resolved, one way
Or another, according to Dodona's priestesses,
Interpreting what Zeus' holy oaks had whispered.
And now this is the hour, the very hour in time,
When we shall see this prophecy fulfilled.
You can hardly be surprised, dear friends, that I should
Start from my sleep, terrified at the thought of finding myself
A widow, parted from the finest man the world has known.

CHORUS.
That's enough now. Hush. Look, that man coming this way.
Is garlanded. He must be bringing good news.

Enter MESSENGER.

MESSENGER.
180   Deianira, my mistress, let me be the first
To free you from your fears. Alcmena's son lives.
He has won a great battle and with the spoils of war
He'll soon return to give his country's gods their share.

DEIANIRA.
Is it true? Tell me, old man. Is this the truth?

MESSENGER.
It's true enough. Crowned with victory. Triumphant.
Your much-respected husband will soon be home.

DEIANIRA.
Who told you this? A citizen or a stranger?

MESSENGER.
Lichas, the herald, is broadcasting it to the world,
Down in the summer pasture. I heard him
190   And hurried here to be the first to let you know
And win your thanks, perhaps even a small reward.

DEIANIRA.
If all is really well, why doesn't Lichas come himself?

MESSENGER.
He's finding it difficult to go anywhere,
My lady. The whole of Trachis, so it seems,
Surrounds him, asking questions. He can hardly move.
Everyone wants to hear the news. They won't release him.
Whatever he wants, they must hear what they want.
You'll see nothing of him until he's satisfied
Their curiosity. Then, I'm sure, he'll come.

DEIANIRA.
Oh Zeus, God of the uncut fields of Oeta,   200
Praise be that after so much time you bring me joy.
This news is the more welcome taking me by surprise.
Sing out in chorus, women, sing it indoors and out.
Sing all of you how day has dawned when least expected.

CHORUS.
Rejoice and sing
From hearth and home.
Come, girl, come,
Sing and rejoice.
Join with the men,
As they sing the praise   210
Of Lord Apollo,
Bowman, protector.

And raise our song
For the maid of Ortygia,
Apollo's sister,
Oh my sisters,
Joined with the nymphs,
Singing the praise
Of Lady Artemis,
Torch-bearer, huntress.   220

I am losing my mind, the flute commands my soul.
Watch me, see me spinning out of control.
The twining ivy makes me Dionysus' slave.
Look, lady, how my joy takes living shape in song.

DEIANIRA.
> I am looking, dear friends, and I can also see
> A group of people who seem to be coming this way.

Enter LICHAS *with a group of* WOMEN CAPTIVES.

DEIANIRA.
> Herald, you're welcome, especially if the news
> You bring, though long delayed, is worth the waiting for.

LICHAS.
> A friendly greeting, madam, and suitably so,
230   Considering my news. A civilised reception
> Should always reward a man who does his best.

DEIANIRA.
> First, dear friend, first you must tell me please
> Whether I shall welcome my Heracles home alive.

LICHAS.
> Of course you will. When I left him he was flourishing,
> Alive, certainly, thriving, bursting with health.

DEIANIRA.
> But where is he? Is he still abroad? You must tell me.

LICHAS.
> On Euboea, the coast of Euboea, setting up an altar
> Where he can dedicate the first-fruits to Cenaean Zeus.

DEIANIRA.
> Is he fulfilling a vow or was there some oracle?

LICHAS.
240   It was a vow he made when he first declared war
> Against that country, whose women you see here before
>   you.

DEIANIRA.
> Who are they? And whose property, god help them?
> I can't pretend I don't feel pity when I look at them.

LICHAS.
> After Eurytus' city had been sacked by Heracles,
> He picked out this lot for himself or for the gods.

DEIANIRA.

>   Was it in order to capture that city that he
>   Stayed away – heaven knows how long?

LICHAS.

>   Not a bit of it. Much of the time he was detained
>   In Lydia, involuntarily, so I hear,
>   Sold into slavery. It would hardly be fair,   250
>   My lady, to blame him for something Zeus ordained.
>   He had to undergo a year, as he told me,
>   In submission to the barbaric Queen Omphale.
>   He was so ashamed of this and so incensed
>   That he swore an oath, promising himself
>   That when he was free, he would enslave in turn
>   The man responsible and his wife and child.
>   He's a man of his word. No sooner had he atoned
>   For his crime than he raised an expeditionary force
>   Against Eurytus, whose fault he thought it was   260
>   Beyond all others, for what he'd had to endure.
>   He had come to Eurytus' house as a former guest,
>   A friend of long standing, but was greeted with reproaches,
>   Pure malice from a poisoned mind. Saying things like
>   'You think you can't miss with those arrows of yours.
>   My sons are better archers than you ever were.' Or again,
>   'Listen to the broken slave talking like a freeman.'
>   Once, Heracles got a little drunk at dinner
>   And Eurytus threw him out the house. That's why
>   When Heracles encountered Iphitus, Eurytus' son,   270
>   Tracking horses on the slopes above Tiryns,
>   He was so incensed he grabbed the distracted boy
>   And hurled him headlong over the towering cliff.
>   Our lord and master, Zeus, father of Olympus,
>   Was angered by the violence of this act.
>   Implacable, he sent Heracles to be sold
>   For killing the young man so treacherously.
>   If the fight had been fair, then Zeus would have judged his case
>   A just one and pardoned him for any offence.
>   But gods, like men, have no fondness for arrogance.   280
>   So, all that overweening, loud-mouthed crew are now
>   First citizens of Hades, down to the very last man.

It's a slave city. These women that you see here
Are finding how high estate can quickly change to low.
They're all yours. Your husband charged me to deliver them
And that's what I've done, exactly as he prescribed.
He will, of course, be here himself the moment
He's fulfilled his holy vows to father Zeus
For his victory. Of all the news I bring you,
290   This, I'm sure, must be by far the most welcome.

CHORUS.

You must be so happy, lady, hearing
What has happened and what you can look forward to.

DEIANIRA.

I am happy, of course I am. Isn't it natural?
Good fortune for my husband means the same for me.
Come what may, our fates are linked by Destiny.
All the same, those who take a balanced view of fate
Will know and fear how ill luck stalks prosperity.
I can't help the pity that wells up in me, dear friends,
Seeing these unhappy women here before us,
300   Bereft of parents, home and country, desolate.
Maybe their fathers were free men until recently.
Now they're condemned to a life of slavery.
You, the god who turns the tide in war, please, Zeus,
Save me from the sight of any child of mine so doomed.
Or, if it has to happen, let me be dead before it does.
The sight of these poor women is terrifying.
Tell me – you look so unhappy – who are you?
Do you have a husband, a child maybe? Looking at you,
I doubt it. You're a child yourself and nobly born.
310   Lichas, who is this girl?
Who was her mother? Tell me. What's her father's name?
Well? I feel the greatest pity looking at her.
She seems the only one who's aware what's happening.

LICHAS.

How should I know? No use asking me. I suppose
It's possible she has more breeding than the rest.

DEIANIRA.

Royal blood? Did Eurytus have a daughter?

LICHAS.
    I have no idea. We never cross-examined her.

DEIANIRA.
    And you never heard the others call her by name?

LICHAS.
    Never. There was a job and I did it. With my mouth shut.

DEIANIRA.
    Poor girl, please tell me what your name is.   320
    It distresses me not to know who you are.

LICHAS.
    If you get a peep out of her it will be a miracle.
    Up to now, I assure you, she hasn't uttered a word,
    Not a single word, good or bad, to anyone.
    She does a lot of weeping. Most of the time she's spent
    Lamenting her misfortunes from the moment she left
    Her windswept homeland. Poor thing. It's hard on her.
    But that's the way it's taken her. Make allowances.

DEIANIRA.
    Let her be. Let her go indoors now.
    Whatever she pleases. I wouldn't want to be responsible   330
    For adding to her present load of misery.
    Enough's enough. We'll all retire indoors.
    I'll not waste your time if you have things to do,
    While I make my domestic preparations.

        Exeunt LICHAS *and the* CAPTIVES.

MESSENGER.
    If you've a moment . . . I can actually tell you
    Privately who those women are you've welcomed.
    No one has said anything to you, but I think you ought to hear
    Exactly what's going on.

DEIANIRA.
    What do you mean? You're standing in my way.

MESSENGER.
    Wait a moment. Hear me out. The news I brought before   340
    Was worth listening to. And, so, I think, is this.

DEIANIRA.

> I'd better call the others back again, shall I?
> Or is this only for me and these women here?

MESSENGER.

> Just us, I think. Better forget the rest.

DEIANIRA.

> Very well then. They've gone. So, what do you want to say?

MESSENGER.

> He's not telling the truth, not strictly anyway.
> Either what he just told you is a fabrication,
> Or his previous report to us was inaccurate.

DEIANIRA.

> What do you mean? I want to know what's going on.
> 350   I can't follow these insinuations.

MESSENGER.

> He said before – I heard him say it myself
> And there's no lack of witnesses – that this girl
> Was the sole reason Heracles made war on Eurytus
> And razed the walled city of Oechalia.
> The God of Love's the only one responsible
> For the hostilities. No Lydians. No slaving for Queen Omphale.
> No punishment for throwing Iphitus off a cliff,
> But Love – that had no part in Lichas' version of events.
> The fact is that Heracles, finding a father
> 360   Loath to sanction his daughter's illicit affair,
> Manufactured some excuse to pick a quarrel
> And brought an army to attack the land
> Of which, as Lichas said, Eurytus was the king.
> And Heracles did kill the girl's father, razing
> His city. Now, madam, as you see, she's joined your household,
> Casually sent ahead, but don't delude yourself.
> She's not here as a slave. He has other plans for her,
> As you might expect, with him so fired by passion.
> I felt I had to tell you everything, madam,
> 370   As I chanced to hear it from Lichas himself.
> There was no lack of witnesses in the market-square,
> People of Trachis, who heard the same as I did

And will testify to it. I'm deeply sorry
If what I've said upsets you. But it is the truth.

DEIANIRA.

Oh no. What can I do? What have I done?
What canker have I welcomed into my home
Without realising? What a fool I am.
How could I think her of no account, anonymous,
As her escort claimed, when she's so beautiful?

MESSENGER.

She's famous, all right. Eurytus was her father.   380
They call her Iole. If Lichas can't tell you that,
It can only be because he never asked her.

CHORUS.

A curse on everyone like that, a curse especially
On deceivers, stirring up trouble, stealthily.

DEIANIRA.

What am I to do? Help me, friends, help me.
All this I've heard, I'm going out of my mind.

CHORUS.

Go and ask Lichas. Perhaps it will all become clear
If you confront him and make him tell the truth.

DEIANIRA.

Yes, you're right. I'll go and fetch him.

MESSENGER.

Do you want me to stay? What do you want me to do?   390

DEIANIRA.

You can stay. We won't have to summon him.
Here he comes from the house of his own accord.

   Enter LICHAS.

LICHAS.

My lady, what message do you have for Heracles?
As you see, I'm leaving. So tell me now.

DEIANIRA.

Leaving? You took long enough to get here. Now
You're taking off before we've had a proper talk.

LICHAS.
  I am still here if there's anything you want to ask.

DEIANIRA.
  Do you think of yourself as a truthful sort of man?

LICHAS.
  Certainly, as God's my witness. As far as I know.

DEIANIRA.
400 Who's the girl, the one you brought just now?

LICHAS.
  Some Euboean. Who her parents are I can't say.

MESSENGER.
  Listen, you. Who do you think you're talking to?

LICHAS.
  May I ask what right you have to speak to me like that?

MESSENGER.
  I'd advise you to answer if you have any sense.

LICHAS.
  I am prepared to answer any questions put to me
  By Deianira, Oeneus' daughter and lord Heracles' wife.
  She's my mistress unless I'm much mistaken.

MESSENGER.
  Right, I'm glad to hear you admit it.
  You're in service to Deianira, agreed?

LICHAS.
                                        I said so.

MESSENGER.
410 Well then. What sort of punishment would you deserve
  If you were found out and proved a hypocrite?

LICHAS.
  A hypocrite? I don't know what you mean.

MESSENGER.
  Don't you? You're the one who's been mincing words.

LICHAS.
I'm off. I was a fool to listen in the first place.

MESSENGER.
Not until you answer one question. It's a brief one.

LICHAS.
If you're so fond of the sound of your own voice, fire away.

MESSENGER.
That prisoner you sent into the house,
You know who I mean?

LICHAS.
I know whom you mean. What about
her?

MESSENGER.
Didn't you say that this girl you can't identify
Was Eurytus' own daughter, Iole?   420

LICHAS.
When did I say that? Who to? Where's your witness?
Who ever heard me say anything like that?

MESSENGER.
Plenty of witnesses down in the town. There was a great crowd
Heard you announce it in the public square in Trachis.

LICHAS.
They can say they heard it. They can say anything they like.
But hearsay report is hardly evidence.

MESSENGER.
'Hearsay report' is it? Didn't you swear an oath
That you brought this girl as a bride for Heracles?

LICHAS.
Bride, do you say I said? Dear lady, for God's sake,
Who is this man? I've never even met him.   430

MESSENGER.
I was there. I heard you. I heard your whole story,
How a city was sacked all for the love of this girl –
Lust rather, but nothing to do with the Lydian queen.

LICHAS.

Send the fellow packing, madam. He must be sick.
There's no point listening to a madman.

DEIANIRA.

No. By Zeus who hurls his thunderbolts across
The tree-lined slopes of Oeta, I want the truth.
You are not addressing some craven creature,
Nor someone ignorant of human nature.
440 I realise that affections may not remain constant.
Only a fool would oppose the God of Love.
To take on Eros would be mere shadow-boxing.
He numbers gods among his victims. Me too.
And if me, why not any other woman like me?
To blame my husband for succumbing to this disease
Would put me as much at fault. Sheer foolishness.
Or to treat the poor girl as though she were the cause.
She's done nothing wrong. I can't say she's wronged me.
It's not like that. But if you've learnt deception from him,
450 For both pupil and teacher the lesson is unjust.
If self-taught, then I must tell you straight,
However well-meaning, what you did was wrong.
Tell me the truth. Hold nothing back. The real disgrace
Is for a free man to have himself branded a liar.
That you could get away with it is inconceivable.
There are quite enough people you talked to who will tell me.
If for some reason you're afraid, there's no need.
Not knowing the truth upsets me, I'll admit,
So what harm in knowing? Do you think there haven't been
            others,
460 Other women in the life of a man like Heracles?
But never has one of them received a reproach from me,
Not a word of blame. Neither shall this girl here,
Even if she was consumed with passion for him.
When I first saw her all I felt was pity.
Nothing can so destroy a life as beauty.
She would not willingly have seen her country overrun,
Poor thing, her people sold as slaves. What's past is past,
Water under the bridge. For the present though,
However you may treat others, don't play me false.

CHORUS.

    You should obey her. Her advice makes sense.   470
    If you take it, she'll thank you, and so will we.

LICHAS.

    Now that I realise, madam, your humanity,
    Your sympathy for human weakness,
    I'll tell you the truth, holding nothing back.
    He's right. Everything's exactly as he said.
    The desire for the girl which overwhelmed Heracles
    Was uncontrollable. Because of it, because of her,
    Her home, Oechalia, was flattened to the ground.
    And, in his defence, I must point out
    He neither tried to hide it, nor told me to.   480
    That was my fault, madam, mine alone, from concern
    In case you might find the truth upsetting.
    If trying to protect you was wrong, then I was wrong.
    But now that the whole story is out in the open,
    For both your sakes, his no less than yours,
    I think you should bear with her and honour
    The reception you gave her when she arrived.
    Your husband may be the best man-at-arms in the world,
    But he met his match when he fell for this girl.

DEIANIRA.

    I think you're right. I'll do as you suggest.   490
    What point is there in inflaming his desire
    By challenging the gods? We'll go inside now.
    I want to write a letter, which you must take
    Along with presents in exchange for his,
    Gift for gift. It wouldn't be right to take nothing back,
    And return empty-handed when you brought so much.

     Exeunt all but the CHORUS.

CHORUS.

    The power of Aphrodite is irresistible.
    No need to talk
    Of Gods' affairs,
    Still less Zeus' own: 500
    No mention of Hades dark as the pit,
    Nor of the earth-shaker,

Lord Poseidon.
Shall I not sing instead
Of two mortal champions,
Rival suitors for one bride,
Raining blows, raising the dust, antagonists?

The power of one of them was a river's power,
A power horned
510 As well as hooved,
Shaped like a bull,
Achelous of Oeneadrae:
And opposite to him
Lord Heracles,
Supreme with bow and club,
From Dionysus' Thebes.
Rivals fighting for one mate,
With referee and marriage-broker, Aphrodite.

The twang of a bow,
520 The blow of a fist,
Locking of horns:
Grapplings and batterings,
Contortions and groanings,
As they clash head to head.
And a gentle girl,
So fair of face,
Sits on the hillside waiting for a husband.
The battle rages
While, scarcely weaned,
530 The girl-prize waits.

Enter DEIANIRA with a box.

DEIANIRA.
My friends, while Lichas is in the house as our guest,
Talking to the captives until it's time to leave,
I've come outside to share a secret with you.
I want to tell you what I've been working at.
After all I've been through, I hope you're sympathetic.
This girl – this mistress would be more appropriate –
I've taken her in, like a captain who takes on a cargo
Despite the fact he fears it. I must be going mad.

Now we are to lie here waiting for him, two lovers
In the one pair of sheets. That is what Heracles,   540
My kind and faithful Heracles as I used to call him,
Offers me in return for all my years of service.
And yet I can't bring myself to be angry with him.
It's a sickness with him and he's been sick like this before.
But how can I share my home with another woman,
Share a marriage with her, share the same bed?
I look at her and she's young. Her beauty's just blooming,
While mine begins to fade. It's the flower that catches the eye.
When it's past its best, a man's footsteps start to wander.
What frightens me is that Heracles, my husband,   550
May call me wife, but the young one will be his woman.
However, as I say, a wife has to be sensible.
Anger will get me nowhere. And here, dear friends,
I have the answer. Let me show you my deliverer.
A long time ago, when I was young, Nessus the Centaur,
A wild shaggy creature, presented me
With a gift that I kept in a bronze container,
A cupful of blood from his wound as he lay dying.
He used to act as ferryman on the Euenus.
He needed neither oar nor sail, not even a boat,   560
But carried people for money, straight through the rapids.
He carried me, when I first left home
To go with Heracles as his new bride.
I was riding on his shoulders when in mid-stream
He started to fondle me. I screamed.
Heracles turned
And planted an arrow straight into his lungs,
Right through the chest. As the creature lay dying,
He gasped out these words: 'Daughter of ancient Oeneus,
Pay heed to what I say and this shall be your reward   570
For being the very last of all my passengers.
Scoop up the blood congealing round my wound,
There where the poison on his arrows, drained
From the Lernaean hydra, has discoloured it.
Keep it and it will serve you as a charm
For Heracles, to make sure he never looks at
Another woman, preferring her to you.'
I thought of this just now, my friends. Since the creature's death

I've kept the stuff safe, hidden away in the house.
580 Before he died he told me how to anoint
A tunic with the blood. Here it is. I've done it.
I've never taken even calculated risks,
Nor could I ever learn to. I hate those who do.
But as for a love-philtre to work on Heracles,
I'll beat this child by a charm if I have to.
Anyway, it's done. I haven't done something stupid, have I?
I think I'm right, but if you don't agree, I won't try it.

CHORUS.
If you're quite sure it's going to work,
I can't see the harm in it. Your reasoning is sound.

DEIANIRA.
590 I can't guarantee it will work. It's never been tried.
I've no reason to doubt how powerful it may be.

CHORUS.
You'll only find out by using it, that's for sure.
Anything else can only be guesswork.

DEIANIRA.
We'll find out soon enough. Here comes Lichas.
He'll be leaving shortly.
Only keep this to yourselves, will you, please?
If what I do is shameful, I don't want my shame public.

Enter LICHAS.

LICHAS.
Have you any instructions, daughter of Oeneus?
Tell me now. I've delayed too long already.

DEIANIRA.
600 While you've been talking to those women indoors,
This is what I have been doing, Lichas,
Preparing a full-length tunic for you to take
As a present for my husband from his wife's own hand.
Make sure he receives it and tell him without fail
That no one else must try it on.
On no account must it be exposed to sunlight
Nor to the light or heat from a sacred hearth

Until he stands up in full view of everyone
On a sacrificial day, to show the Gods.
I promised myself as soon as I should see him   610
Back home, or at least hear that he was safe,
To dress him in this tunic, put him on display
In the glorious robe, an offering to the Gods.
I'll put my seal to the lock, impress it with my signet,
So he'll know the box was sent by me.
Away you go now and make sure you take care this time
Not to let your tongue exceed your authority.
That way he will thank you and so will I,
And you will have earned double thanks.

LICHAS.

Hermes, god of messengers, attend me.   620
If I follow his craft as I should, I will serve you truly,
Delivering this casket exactly as it is,
And faithfully repeating your message, word for word.

DEIANIRA.

You may go. I presume you are aware
Of how things stand, domestically.

LICHAS.

I am, yes, and I'll tell him all is well.

DEIANIRA.

And you know, because you saw it, about the girl.
How I received her and welcomed her here.

LICHAS.

I was delighted, madam, as well as surprised.

DEIANIRA.

That's it then. Is there anything else to tell him?   630
I'm wary of saying how much I want to see him
Before I find out if he still wants me.

Exeunt severally LICHAS *and* DEIANIRA.

CHORUS.

All you who live your lives
By the warm springs and the rocky sanctuary
Of Oeta,

By the Malian gulf
And by the shoreline of the golden-bowed Artemis,
There where the Council meets,
Famed throughout Greece,

640   The mellifluous flute
Will soon enough be heard again amongst you,
Not sombre,
But lyrical, lyre-like.
Heracles, the son of Zeus and Alcmena,
Brandishing trophies,
Is coming home.

Twelve months we have waited,
Enduring his absence,
The drifter adrift.
650   While at home and lamenting,
Grief doubling and redoubling,
His poor wife was wasting
Till, moved at last, Ares
Has freed them from misery.

Let him come. Let him come.
Hurry, you great ship
With your rows of oars,
Don't stop till you've brought him here,
Leaving his sacrifice behind
660   At the island altar,
Driven by the passion
From the Centaur's magic charm.

   Enter DEIANIRA.

DEIANIRA.
   Listen, all of you, I'm frightened. I may have gone too far.
   I'm afraid I shouldn't have done what I just did.

CHORUS.
   Deianira, whatever has happened?

DEIANIRA.
   I don't know. But I'm afraid that with the best intentions
   I may have triggered some catastrophe.

CHORUS.
  You don't mean with the gift you sent to Heracles?

DEIANIRA.
  I do, yes. To rush blindly into action
  Without knowing the consequences is so stupid.   670

CHORUS.
  But what are you afraid of? Tell us, if you can.

DEIANIRA.
  Something just happened. If I tell you as friends,
  You'll know I never expected anything so strange.
  I used a tuft of wool, a good piece, white,
  To smear the tunic that I sent him to wear.
  It's disappeared.
  No one indoors got rid of it. It simply disintegrated,
  Shrivelled up by itself where I dropped it on the flags.
  I'll tell you the full story, hold nothing back.
  Everything that the Centaur gasped out to me   680
  As he lay with the arrow in his ribs
  I remembered, precisely as he told it,
  Indelible, as though engraved on bronze.
  I followed those instructions in every detail.
  I was to keep the charm out of harm's way
  Where heat could not reach it from fire or sunlight.
  That way it would stay fresh till I needed it for him.
  So I did. The time came. Just now I pulled out
  A handful of wool from one of the palace sheep
  And took it to my room, privately. I anointed the robe   690
  Carefully, my special present for him, folded it
  And put it safely in the strong-box as you saw.
  But as I was returning indoors, I saw something, maybe an
                                                              omen –
  I don't know how to tell you – something inexplicable.
  I happened to have thrown the piece of wool,
  The piece I smeared the tunic with, down where the sunlight
  Fell full upon it. As it grew warm, then hot,
  It dissolved,
  Till all that was left was a little heap of something
  Like nothing so much as sawdust, lying there.   700

But from the ground on which it had fallen
There started to ooze up bubbles, a mass of bubbles,
Frothing like the blue-black juice when grapes
Have been picked from the vine and crushed underfoot.
I don't know what to do. I think I'm going mad.
What I've seen tells me I've done something monstrous.
Whyever should I think that some wild creature
Would look on me kindly when I had caused his death?
Of course he didn't. He must have been tricking me
710 To get his own back on the man who shot him.
Too late. I see it all now. But it's too late.
Unless I am deceiving myself yet again,
I've killed my own husband, God help me, single-handed.
The arrow that killed Nessus would have killed any
    creature
Who touched it, I know that. It wounded Cheiron
And he was a God. How could I ever think
That the black blood which seeped from Nessus' wound
Would not kill Heracles? It must. I know it will.
Well then, I'm resolved that if he is destroyed,
720 I won't live to see the consequences.
For any woman who truly values virtue,
To live branded evil would be unbearable.

CHORUS.
There's no escaping the fear of disaster,
But don't abandon hope before you know the outcome.

DEIANIRA.
To someone who has made the wrong decision
Hope is a luxury to keep up the spirit.

CHORUS.
But when it's a mistake, as in your case,
The victim's anger is usually moderated.

DEIANIRA.
That's easy for you to say – you're innocent
730 Of complicity – harder for me who has to live with it.

CHORUS.
You'd be advised to say nothing more at present,

Unless you want to say it to your son.
You sent him to look for his father. Here he is back.

Enter HYLLUS.

HYLLUS.
I would want one of three things for you, Mother.
Your death. Alternatively,
That I was someone else's son. Or failing that,
That you were wholly changed from what you are.

DEIANIRA.
Hyllus, what is it? Why do you hate me so?

HYLLUS.
Your husband, Heracles, my father, are you listening?
Today, you killed him.   740

DEIANIRA.
What do you mean?

HYLLUS.
I mean that it's inevitable.
What's done cannot be undone.

DEIANIRA.
How can you say this, Hyllus? Who told you
That I was responsible for this dreadful business?

HYLLUS.
I saw the whole terrible thing, Mother,
With my own eyes. No one told me.

DEIANIRA.
Where did you find him? Were you with him when it happened?

HYLLUS.
If you must know, then I must tell you everything.
When he had sacked the famed city of Eurytus,   750
Laden with trophies and the spoils of victory,
He came to Cenaeum on the wave-washed shore
Of Euboea. There he marked out the space to dedicate
Altars and a sacred grave for his father Zeus.
I was so relieved to see him.

He was planning a multiple sacrifice
When Lichas arrived, his herald, come from home.
Bringing your gift to him, that lethal cloak.
Heracles put it on, as you had prescribed,
760   And proceeded to the sacrifice, killing first
A dozen perfect bulls. Altogether
He sacrificed a hundred beasts of various kinds.
At first light-hearted, revelling in the splendour
Of the robe, he began to pray, poor man.
But when the flames from the sacrifice began to flare,
Bloody and hissing from the pitchy pine-logs,
His skin began to sweat. The tunic was
Sticking to his body, all over him,
As though a craftsman had glued it.
770   A stinging pain tore at his body, bone-deep.
Like snake-venom, it began to feed on him.
He called out for Lichas, poor Lichas,
Who had nothing to do with the suffering you had caused,
Demanding to know what he'd plotted, bringing the tunic.
The wretched fellow knew nothing except that
The gift was yours. You sent it, he delivered it.
While Heracles listened, a spasm shot through him,
Agony clawing at his lungs.
He grabbed Lichas by the foot where the ankle bends at the heel,
780   And smashed him against a rock jutting out of the sea.
And where the skull was broken, hair and blood,
Brains beginning to dribble through, whitely.
Everyone present cried out in horror
At one man suffering, the other who'd lost his life.
No one dared come anywhere near Heracles.
He was writhing on the ground, then stretching full-length.
He was screaming. He was shrieking. The cliffs echoed,
From the headlands of Locris, round the heights of Euboea.
Then the pain passed, but now in his misery
790   He cast himself to the ground, grieving, lamenting,
Reviling the calamity of his marriage
To a malignant wife, meaning you, won as a bride
From Ceneus, to his irrevocable destruction.
He caught sight of me through the swirling smoke,
Fixed me with his eye as I stood there in the crowd,

Tears streaming down my face. Distracted with pain he called
out

'My boy, come here. Don't run away when I'm in trouble
Even if it means your sharing my death with me.
Take me away from here, take me to where
No mortal man can witness what is happening.   800
At least, for pity's sake, take me away,
Away from this land, now. I don't want to die here.'
So he charged me. We found a ship and laid him on the deck,
And headed for home, back to this land, still
Groaning and writhing. Soon you will see him,
Just alive, or just dead.
That, Mother, is what you planned against my father,
And that is how successful you've been. May Justice
And an avenging Fury pay you out. That is my prayer,
If such a prayer can be right. But it must be right,   810
Since you have cast right to the winds by slaughtering
The finest man who ever lived, whose like we'll never see again.

 Exit DEIANIRA.

CHORUS.
 Why do you creep away in silence? Don't you see
 That silence will be taken for a confession?

HYLLUS.
 Let her creep away. As long as it's out of my sight,
 She can creep wherever she wants.
 How could she still deserve a mother's name,
 When there's nothing of the mother in what she's done?
 Creep off. What a triumph. And may she inherit
 The self-same blessing she visited on my father.   820

 Exit HYLLUS.

CHORUS.
 It closes in.
 Watch, sisters,
 How the ancient prophecy
 Suddenly comes true.
 'The twelfth month of the twelfth year
 Shall see an end to the labours

Of Zeus' great son.'
It all ties up.
For how can a man who's lost his life
830   Be asked to serve amongst the dead?

Necessity,
Pain-dealing,
Wraps about his ribs the Centaur's
Bloody winding-sheet,
Steeped in poison, bred by Death,
Stewed in the long-dead hydra-juice.
How shall he see
Another dawn?
Black-maned, sly-speaking, the Centaur
840   Drives him, gnawing at his nerve-ends.

How much of this did the poor woman know?
She knew nothing,
Saw a threat to her marriage,
Her rival a novelty.
The remedy was destructive, but only through her blindness.
Her grief is real enough,
Real the flood of tears
That wets her cheeks.
What's happening brings treachery to light,
850   Impending doom.

And now our tears are flowing. Heracles,
His sickness spreading,
Pitifully faces pain
No enemy could inflict.
Alas for the black spear which won him his battle-bride,
Too hasty a marriage
To his bride from steep
Oechalia.
Now the real cause is revealed,
860   Secret work by
Aphrodite.

SEMI-CHORUS A.
I think I hear –

Fancy maybe –
Someone crying in the palace.
What did I tell you?

SEMI-CHORUS B.
There, clearly.
Something terrible inside.

Enter NURSE.

SEMI-CHORUS A.
Look, the old woman,
Bowed down, down-cast.
Something has happened.   870

NURSE.
Oh, my dears, what a shock of troubles
In the gift she sent to Heracles.

CHORUS.
What are you talking about that we don't already know?

NURSE.
She's left us. Deianira's set out
On the final journey that you take stock-still.

CHORUS.
Not dead. Please, not dead.

NURSE.
                        You heard me.

CHORUS.
Poor woman. Dead?

NURSE.
                        Again, then. Yes, she's dead.

CHORUS.
Poor, poor woman. Can you tell me what happened?

NURSE.
The way she chose was awful.

CHORUS.
                        Tell us anyway.

880 Tell us the worst.

NURSE.
She killed herself.

CHORUS.
What possessed her? What made her do it?

NURSE.
Impaled herself . . .

CHORUS.
How could she heap another death on death?
And all alone?

NURSE.
On the sharp point of a sword.

CHORUS.
Did you see this mad act?

NURSE.
I saw it. I was standing close by.

CHORUS.
Did anyone . . . ? How did she . . . ? Tell me the details.

NURSE.
890 She did it by herself, all by herself.

CHORUS.
Do you expect us to . . . ?

NURSE.
It's the truth.

CHORUS.
That bride, that brand-new bride
Has given birth already,
Given birth to a Fury in this house.

NURSE.
A Fury, yes. And had you been there to witness
What Deianira did, you could only have pitied her.

CHORUS.
But could a woman set her hand to such a deed?

NURSE.

 Oh yes, terrible as it seems. I'll tell you. I was there.
 When she came indoors she was by herself.   900
 She caught sight of her son, Hyllus, getting ready
 A litter, hollowed out, for carrying his father home,
 And went to hide where nobody would see her,
 Throwing herself down, inconsolable, by the altars
 Soon to be neglected for ever. And she wept.
 She wept as she touched the furniture, things she used,
 Rushing here and there, all over the house.
 Catching sight of servants she was fond of,
 She would stare at them, poor thing, and burst into tears,
 Weep at her own ill-starred destiny   910
 And her house condemned to lose its children.
 After that she said no more and I saw her run
 Suddenly to Heracles' bedroom.
 Hidden where she couldn't see me, I watched her
 Take bedclothes and throw them down.
 She was making Heracles' bed.
 And when she'd finished she threw herself on top of it,
 Cowering there in the middle of the bed she'd made,
 Tears streaming down her face. And she talked to it:
 'Dear bed, goodbye. Goodbye, bedroom,   920
 A long goodbye.
 This is the last time that you'll welcome me to sleep.'
 That was all she said. Resolutely, she raised her hand,
 Undid her dress at the brooch over her breast,
 Laying her left side bare
 And her left arm to the elbow.
 Then I ran, ran as fast as my strength allowed
 To tell Hyllus what she was planning to do.
 But in the time it took to find him and get back,
 She took a doubled-bladed sword, as we discovered,   930
 And stabbed herself through the ribs straight to the heart.
 Hyllus screamed when he saw her. He knew, the wretched man,
 That his anger was responsible.
 By now he'd found out from others in the house
 That she was a mere instrument in the Centaur's plan.
 But too late. Poor boy, he's overcome with grief,
 Comfortless, sobbing over her body,

Kissing her, hugging her,
Lying there, crying out
940   That it was he had killed her with his accusation,
And now, all in one day, found himself orphaned,
Deprived of both his father and his mother.
So, there you have it. Only a hare-brained man
Banks on tomorrow or what comes after tomorrow.
There never was, there cannot be tomorrow
Until today is safely yesterday.

    Exit NURSE.

CHORUS.
What grieve for first?
What griefs crowd next?
Help me, my judgement falters.

950   What's there in the house,
What's coming,
What's here, what threatens, which worse?

Oh for a whirlwind
To pick us gently up
And take us away from here.
I'm frightened
That the sight of our illustrious hero
May be too much for me.
They say he's coming home,
960   Wracked, tormented,
Shocking to see, shocking beyond belief.

Now it's upon us,
The sorrow that I sensed
In my song, like a nightingale.
A procession
Of foreigners heading this way. Will they manage,
Shuffling like pall-bearers,
Escorting a friend?
Unconscious or dead?
970   Asleep, or have we already lost him?

Enter HYLLUS, *an* OLD MAN *and* ATTENDANTS *with*
HERACLES *on a litter.*

HYLLUS.
I mourn for you, father,
Mourn for your pain, for my suffering.
God help me, what can I do?

OLD MAN.
Hush, boy, don't excite
Your tormented father's agony.
He's alive, just.
Hold on, bite your lip.

HYLLUS.   Did you say he's still alive?

OLD MAN.
Don't wake him,
Don't provoke him, don't stir up
That fearful frenzy, boy.   980

HYLLUS.
I can't bear it.
I'm losing my mind.

HERACLES.
Oh God,
Where am I? Who are all these people?
I don't know them. Watching me suffer.
Ahh. That hurts.
The fearsome thing gnaws at me.

OLD MAN.
I told you to keep quiet.
I told you not to rouse him,
Chasing the peace of sleep from his eye and mind.   990

HYLLUS.
I couldn't help myself.
I couldn't stand so terrible a sight.

HERACLES.
So this is my reward
For all the sacrifices

Made at Cenaea's altar-steps
This is how you treat me, is it, Zeus?
Would that I had never set eyes on Cenaea,
Or had to face such pain.
Such exquisite, maddening pain.
1000   Is there any sorcerer,
Any surgeon, skilled enough
To free me from the scourge, but Zeus?
To find one would be a miracle.
Ah. Let me be.
Let me sleep,
My final, desperate sleep.

Don't touch me. Where are you putting me?
That kills me. You're killing me.
It was calming down. You've roused it again.
1010   Here it comes. It snatches at me.
You're the vilest of Greeks, if Greeks you really are.
I slaved for you, cleaned up your high seas and your forests.
And is there no one will fetch me fire or a sword
To free me from my suffering?
Will none of you
Cut the head from my body?
Damn you all.

OLD MAN.
Come boy, this task is greater than I can manage.
I haven't the strength. Give me a hand here.
1020   You're fitter to help him than I am.

HYLLUS.
I've got him.
But offering relief from pain,
Out here or indoors, is beyond my power.
This is God's will.

HERACLES.
Hyllus, where are you?
Hyllus? Support me.
Here, here, lift me up. Oh God.
It's savage, savaging me again,
Mercilessly clawing at me,

Murderous, incurable. 1030
Ah Athena, Athena, it's eating me alive.
Pity, Hyllus. Be merciful to your father.
Take your sword – you won't be blamed for it –
And thrust it here into my throat,
The only way to free me
From this agony your godless mother
Has inflicted on me.
May she suffer the same
And may I watch,
Watch her die as I am dying. 1040
Sweet death, brother of Zeus,
Rest me, free me from this torture.
One stroke, quick, sharp, then peace.

CHORUS.
I shrink with horror, dear friends, to hear
How such a man could be so driven by pain.

HERACLES.
These hands, this back, have suffered in the past
Hard work, heated endeavours, evil, truth to tell.
But never like this. Not when Zeus' wife, Hera,
Confronted me, not at the hands of wretched Eurystheus.
Nothing to match the way the daughter of Oeneus, 1050
Two-faced Deianira, has entangled me,
Murdering me, stuck in a Fury's clinging web.
It clings to me, consuming my very innards,
Invading till the breath drains from my lungs,
Guzzling on my fresh blood to the last drop.
My body's wasting away – there'll be nothing left –
Imprison'd in her unspeakable embrace.
No enemy spear could do this on the battlefield,
No earth-born giant, no wild beast,
No Greek, no foreigner anywhere I roamed, 1060
Purging the land as I went. But she did.
One woman, acting as a woman, nothing like a man,
Has downed me, single-handed without even a sword.
Hyllus, you must act now as your father's son
And pay no respect to your mother's name.
I want her. Fetch her yourself from the house

And deliver her into my hands. I need to watch you
While she is suffering to see which grieves you most,
Her pain or mine.

1070 Come on, boy, be brave. I need compassion from you.
Others feel pity enough when they see me howling,
And weeping like a girl. There's no one alive
Can say they saw the like of this before.
Whatever I suffered, I suffered without a murmur.
But this. I've lost my manhood.
Come here. Come on, stand by your father.
Take a good look at this suffering, brought about
By mischance. Off with the coverings. I'll show you.
Now look, all of you, look at this poor body.

1080 Feast your eyes on this miserable, pitiful sight.
Ah, damned pain.
It shoots straight through me.
Through my chest. Consuming pain.
Will it never leave me?
Death take me, I beg you.
Demolish me, Zeus,
With a thunderbolt.
Strike me with lightning, my father. Please.
It's breaking out again, flaming, devouring

1090 My hands and my back, my chest and my arms:
Arms, which overcame the indomitable lion
None of Nemea's herdsmen could stand up to,
Yet you subdued it. The Lernaean hydra too.
And that savage Centaur pack, half-horse, half-man,
Lawless and overbearing, vicious crew that they were.
And the Erymanthian boar and from Hades
Beneath the earth the triple-headed hound,
The whelp of Echidna. What a monster that was.
Irresistible. And at the far ends of the earth,

1100 The dragon, guardian of the golden apples.
These and a hundred others I overcame.
No one took me on and then set up a trophy.
Now look at me, with no use left in my limbs,
A shredded thing, blind Fate's whipping-boy,
Me with a mother well-born enough,
My father Zeus himself, lord of the starry heaven.

But this I swear to you. I may be nothing now,
Unable so much as to crawl, but let me
Get my hands on who's responsible. Let her come here
And I'll show her, show the whole world,   1110
In death, no less than in life, I pay evil back.

CHORUS.
Poor Greece. With the loss of such a man as this,
What grief, what mourning you must undergo.

HYLLUS.
You have spoken, father. Now you're silent.
I know how ill you are, but listen to my response.
I ask nothing else for you but what is right.
Be true to your real self, before you were consumed
With fury from the grinding pain. There's no point
Glorying in revenge for what you have suffered.

HERACLES.
Say anything you like, so long as it's clear.   1120
I'm too sick to play word-games.

HYLLUS.
I have to tell you about mother,
How she is – how she did what she did in error.

HERACLES.
You little wretch. How dare you speak of her,
A murdering mother who has killed your father?

HYLLUS.
I can't keep silent about what I know.

HERACLES.
Nor should you after the crimes that she's committed.

HYLLUS.
What she's done today, you mean?

HERACLES.
Go on then. But take care. You may condemn yourself.

HYLLUS.
You have to know. She's dead. A short while ago.   1130

HERACLES.
Who killed her? Strange. I don't like the sound of this.

HYLLUS.
By her own hand. She killed herself.

HERACLES.
Too soon. I ought to have killed her myself.

HYLLUS.
Even you would soften, if only you knew.

HERACLES.
An odd thing to say. Knew what?

HYLLUS.
Briefly. She did wrong. But she meant well.

HERACLES.
'Meant well', did she, damn you, when she murdered your
father?

HYLLUS.
She thought she was giving you a love-charm.
It was a mistake. She'd seen your brand-new wife.

HERACLES.
1140   Who in Trachis could have given her a love-charm?

HYLLUS.
Ages ago the Centaur, Nessus, told her
She could rekindle your love by using a charm.

HERACLES.
Nessus. Ah, Nessus, damn him. I might have known.
I'm finished. Done for. Out goes the light.
Now I know. I see it all.
Come here, my boy, come. This is the end for your father.
Go and fetch your brothers, all the family,
Alcmena too, poor Alcmena, loved by Zeus –
What a waste. My parting words to you
1150   Shall be prophecies I know and you must hear.

HYLLUS.
Your mother's not here. She went to the coast,

To Tiryns. That's where she lives now.
Some of the boys are with her. She looks after them.
And I have to tell you some of us live in Thebes.
Those of us who are here, father, will follow
Your instructions as thoroughly as we can.

HERACLES.

Listen then. Listen carefully. The time has come
For you to show whether or not you're any son of mine.
It was prophesied by my father long ago
That no man alive would cause my death,   1160
But some resident of Hell, a dead creature.
The Centaur was that creature. It all turned out
According to god's word. The dead kill the living.
There was another oracle following on the first.
Of course. They match, the first, then this.
Up in the mountains where the Selli live
And sleep on the ground, I heard my father's prophecy,
Delivered in the rustling of the oak-groves.
I wrote what he said, that in due time
I'd find release from all the labours that oppressed me.   1170
That time is now.
A happy release is what he meant, not happiness.
The dead are free from labour.
It's obvious, Hyllus, that's what's happening.
And you have a part to play. You must help me.
No hesitating. Don't provoke me now.
You alone can do what we have to do.
Remember this rule as golden. Obey your father.

HYLLUS.

What you say worries me, father. I don't know
What you have in mind but I'll do it. I'll obey.   1180

HERACLES.

Give me your right hand.

HYLLUS.

Why do you need such a promise?

HERACLES.

Don't cross me. Your hand. Quick.

HYLLUS.
  It's all right. Here.

HERACLES.
  Swear. On the head of my father, Zeus. Swear.

HYLLUS.
  Swear what? Aren't you going to tell me?

HERACLES.
  That you'll do what I tell you to do.

HYLLUS.
  As Zeus is my witness. I swear.

HERACLES.
  And a curse on your head if you withdraw.

HYLLUS.
1190   That isn't necessary. I'll do it. Oh, very well.

HERACLES.
  Right. You know the highest peak on Oeta, sacred to Zeus.

HYLLUS.
  I know it. I've sacrificed up there many times.

HERACLES.
  You must carry my body up there, yourself,
  With help from your friends, if you need it.
  Then cut down wood, lots of it,
  Mature oak with deep roots, wild olive,
  Then you must lay my body on top,
  Light a pine torch and set it on fire.
  No weeping, not a single tear.
1200   Dry-eyed, I'll have no signs of mourning.
  That's if you really are a son of mine.
  If you don't do it, I'll come back and haunt you.

HYLLUS.
  Father, what are you saying? That's a terrible thing, you're
                                                        asking.

HERACLES.
  It has to be done. And if you refuse,

Don't call me father. I disown you.

HYLLUS.
    Dear God. You're asking me to murder you.
    Polluted. Parricide, that's what they'll call me.

HERACLES.
    No. No. My doctor. The means, the only means
    By which my suffering can be cured.

HYLLUS.
    How can I cure your body by burning it?   1210

HERACLES.
    If you're afraid of that, at least do everything else.

HYLLUS.
    I'll carry you there. Of course.

HERACLES.
    And build the pyre, just as I said.

HYLLUS.
    As long as I don't actually have to lay my hands on it.
    I'll do everything else. You needn't worry about that.

HERACLES.
    All right. I'm satisfied. There is one thing.
    One extra favour on top of all you've done.

HYLLUS.
    You've only to ask, whatever it is.

HERACLES.
    You know that girl, Eurytus' daughter?

HYLLUS.
    Iole, you mean?   1220

HERACLES.
    Oh you do know her. Well, my son, this is my request.
    It's to do with her. When I am dead – remember
    You did swear an oath to do whatever I said –
    I want you to marry her. Now, don't let your father down.
    I slept with her. Iole. She's lain by my side.
    I don't want anyone else to have her

Except you, my boy. Take her as your bride.
Please. Do as I say. All these great things you've agreed
Will be cancelled out if you won't humour me in this.

HYLLUS.

1230   How can I be angry with someone so sick?
But who could tolerate a thing like that?

HERACLES.

Does all that muttering mean you won't?

HYLLUS.

How could anyone agree? That's the girl who single-handed
Caused my mother's death and the state you're in.
I'd have to be possessed to marry her.
Father, to die alongside you would be better
Than to live in the same house as our enemy.

HERACLES.

So, this fellow, it appears, will not respect
A father's dying request. God's curse awaits you

1240   If you fail to keep faith with everything I said.

HYLLUS.

Calm yourself. You'll have a relapse if you're not careful.

HERACLES.

It's your fault, stirring up my sleeping demon.

HYLLUS.

Damned. I'm damned, whichever way I turn.

HERACLES.

Because you won't listen to what your father fairly asks.

HYLLUS.

Fairly? You've only wickedness to teach me.

HERACLES.

How can it be wicked if it's what I want?

HYLLUS.

Are you sure it would be right to do what you say?

HERACLES.

Of course it would be right. The gods are my witnesses.

HYLLUS.
    I'll do it. With the gods' approval,
    I'll not hold back. Anything's better, father,   1250
    Than appearing to break my word to you.

HERACLES.
    At last. Thank heaven. Now, quick as you can,
    Pick me up and take me to the fire
    Before another spasm overtakes me.
    Lift me. Hurry now.
    Peace at last and an end for Heracles.

HYLLUS.
    There's nothing to stop me, father,
    Obeying your orders now. You force me to it.

HERACLES.
    On then. Be resolute, my soul.
    Before the pain floods back,   1260
    Lips set like stone, steely, muzzling,
    Muffling the scream,
    Grudging but the end is triumph.

HYLLUS.
    Raise him aloft as you carry him.
    Forgive me my complicity.
    The Gods, not men, are the true cause,
    Of everything that happens,
    Claiming a father's respect
    But overlooking all our suffering.
    No mortal man can see the future,   1270
    The present's bad enough.
    For all this suffering here,
    The cruellest fate that any man endured,
    The Gods should be ashamed.

    You too, women of Trachis, away from this house.
    For you have witnessed strange and terrible deaths,
    Horrors never seen before.
    Zeus' fault. All of it. The fault of Zeus.

Electra and *Philoctetes* – A Note on the Translation

Twenty-five years ago, when I published my first Sophocles translations, the view was still current among classical scholars that no one 'deserved' Sophocles who couldn't read Greek, and that translations betrayed a sacred trust. This view still persists in the dimmer regions of academe, but there is now, thankfully, agreement everywhere else that Sophocles belongs to everyone and not just to a narrow and self-protective clique. Translations are essential tools: not rivals of the original (as anyone who has read Shakespeare in French or German will agree) but a useful and, for most of their readers, essential substitute.

Translators of Sophocles need to bear this fact in mind. We must not write with one eye watching out for scholarly knives. We must write for English speakers, English readers – and, perhaps most vitally, English-speaking actors. And we should be adept at handling not so much the language we are working from, as our own. Anyone, given patience, can learn enough Greek to read, and construe, Sophocles. Choosing appropriate English is a subtler and rarer skill. As I translate, I spend only a fraction of the time puzzling out what each line means; the bulk of my effort goes into trying to express that meaning in English which will make a similar, and similarly forceful, effect.

I think that this is especially important in drama. The words actors speak are just one part of the totality of a performance, and Sophocles, as he wrote, had the whole effect in mind. He knew, so to say, what his actors might do with each and every line. The author of a modern published translation is working for a wider group of people: readers, school students looking for cribs (who may be disappointed if a translation is halfway any good), performers not at a single festival but in many theatres and at many times. The translated text has to be much more flexible, more general, than the original. It has to be not so much an exact portrait as a construction kit, from which each user can assemble his or her idea of what Sophocles had in mind.

One major problem is the split, in all Sophocles' surviving plays, between language and emotion. Sophocles was, it seems to me, particularly interested in subversion and in the presentation of extreme states of mind. His characters are racked, first by the need to make choices depending on their understanding of the situation and of themselves, and second by the need to endure the consequences of what they choose. He is less interested in the moment of choice itself, than in the turmoil which lies on either side of it. His characters' world is chaotic, plagued with hints and ironies, and dangerous. And yet he defines it, and them, in language which is simple, pellucid and almost dandyishly neat. No words are baroque (as half Aeschylus' vocabulary is); no thoughts are bizarre (as many of Euripides' images are); not one sentence, not a single phrase, would make Beckmesser sniff.

Faced with this Jekyll and Hyde quality in their author, translators, too, must choose. One can render Sophocles fairly literally, using rhythms close to his, keeping the line lengths and leaving nothing out. This approach avoids interpretation: it leaves the reader or performer to flesh out meaning, style and pace. The risk is blandness – false to Sophocles. Another approach is to interpret vigorously as you go along, to cut, adapt, reorder – in fact to write your own play based on Sophocles. This may be fun – Ezra Pound's *Women of Trachis* is amazing – and it may enthral readers, but it is also false to Sophocles.

In my own translations I try to steer a middle course. I know that my versions will be staged and that actors and directors will take them to pieces and reassemble them in the way all good performers do. I try not to overemphasise my own interpretation of what Sophocles meant, to leave room for alternative visions. But I also know that people will read my translations quietly from books, at home. They do not interpret; they absorb, and they need a few pointers to what Sophocles' original, in my opinion, was about. Where his verse made a particular effect (for example by being rhythmically 'perfect' or by using assonance, strings of polysyllables or short, stabbing sentences), I try to do the same. I try to make the way the English falls serve the purposes of irony, as the Greek so often does – a good example is the Servant's description of the chariot-race in *Electra*, deliberately intended (by the Servant) to be a performance, and (by Sophocles) to sound slightly artificial, just a little over the top. I try to make the Choruses more elliptical than the dialogue, even though this can make them hard to read. (Paradoxically, in every performance where the nettle is grasped and the Choruses are sung, they work perfectly, both in their own right and as balance-points within the show.)

It is for each reader, each performer, to judge how successful any translation is at unpacking and revealing the author it serves. Translators should be proud of what they do – it is after all a craft, a creative art. But they should also be humble. At the London Press Night of my version of *Philoctetes*, someone led me to a critic saying 'Do let me introduce you to the author'. Both the critic and I looked round with a wild surmise – but the old man, alas, had slipped away.

Kenneth McLeish, 1990

ELECTRA

Translated by Kenneth McLeish

Characters

ORESTES
ELECTRA
PYLADES
CHRYSOTHEMIS
CLYTEMNESTRA
AEGISTHUS
SERVANT OF ORESTES, an old man
SLAVES
CHORUS OF THE WOMEN OF ARGOS

This translation of *Electra* was performed in London by the
Royal Shakespeare Company in 1989, with the following cast:

SERVANT OF ORESTES	Sylvester Morant
ORESTES	Piers Ibbotson
PYLADES	Derek Hutchinson
ELECTRA	Fiona Shaw
CHRYSOTHEMIS	Susan Colverd
CLYTEMNESTRA	Natasha Parry
AEGISTHUS	Gordon Case
CHORUS	Darlene Johnson,
	Kate Littlewood, Franchine Mulrooney,
	Sonia Ritter, Julia Swift

Directed by Deborah Warner

An open courtyard outside the palace of Mycenae in Argos. In the background, the palace doors.

Enter a SERVANT, ORESTES *and* PYLADES.

SERVANT.

Orestes, son of Agamemmon, son
Of the warlord who led the Greeks at Troy,
We are in Argos – the ancient land
You pined for, and longed to see again.
Look, over there: the sacred plain
Of Io, child of the river-god;
Down there, the Lycean Agora, named
For Lycean Apollo; there, on our left,
The famous temple of Hera. This place,
Where we are standing now, is Mycenae –
Golden Mycenae, rich in death,   10
Palace of the dynasty of Pelops.
When they butchered your father, I took you
Away from here, on the orders of Electra
Your sister. I saved you, I brought you up
To manhood, to avenge your father's death.

Orestes, and Pylades dearest of friends,
We must make our plans at once.
The dark blanket of stars is put away,
And birds are carolling the rising sun.
Before anyone stirs, it is time to talk.   20
Our long waiting is over: now we must act.

ORESTES.

My faithful friend, everything you do,
Every word you say, proclaims your loyalty.
Just as a thoroughbred shows its mettle
Even in old age, pricking its ears
And snorting at danger, so you are first
With good advice, first with encouragement.
This is my plan. Listen carefully,   30
And if I miss the target, guide my aim.

I went to consult Apollo's oracle,
To ask the god how I was to avenge
My father and punish his murderers.
This was the answer:

113

'Go yourself, helped by no army.
Use tricks to snatch the punishment.
They killed; they must die.'

The god's oracle was clear; we must obey.
When the moment comes, you must find a way
40   To get inside the palace and spy on them.
Bring back a clear report. No one inside
Will recognise you after all these years.
An old man with white hair – who will suspect?
Tell them this story. You are a visitor
From Phocis, sent by the lord Phanoteus,
Their most trusted ally. You bring news –
And this you must confirm with a solemn oath –
That Orestes is dead, in an accident
At the Pythian Games:
In the chariot-race, he was thrown and killed.
50   Make that your story. While you are telling it,
The two of us will visit my father's grave,
As Apollo commanded. We shall make
Tomb-offerings: wine, and a cut lock of hair.
Then we'll come back, bringing the bronze urn
You know of, hidden in the wood – and trick
Our enemies with the glad news they long for,
That my body is burnt to ash, and gone.
60   A bad omen, to call the living dead?
By pretending death I live again;
I avenge my father, and win fame.
Deeds, not words – there's nothing to fear.
There are stories of wise men of old
Who pretended death and came to life again,
Reborn to glory greater than before.
So I shall be born from pretended death,
A new, bright star to scorch my enemies.

O Argos my country, O gods of home,
Welcome me! Smile on my journey!
O palace of Agamemnon my father,
70   I have come, with the gods, to end this plague –
Don't drive me away! My own kingdom –
Let me restore it, and win the throne!

God grant my prayers. And now, to work, old man.
You know your orders: see they are obeyed.
We'll go, and play our part. For all of us
The moment of fate is now: we must use it well.

ELECTRA (*inside*).
O Zeus! Zeus!

SERVANT.
Orestes, listen! Someone's crying . . .
There, inside. Some unhappy slave-girl.

ORESTES.
Or else my sister, unhappy Electra.   80
Shall we stay here a moment, and listen?

SERVANT.
No: we must put Apollo's orders first.
Hurry to Agamemnon's grave, and make
The offerings. That is the surest way
To win success, and bring us victory.

They go. Enter ELECTRA. As she speaks, the Chorus of
WOMEN OF ARGOS *also enters.*

ELECTRA.
Light of the morning,
Sky-canopy above,
As the shadows of night
Melt into day, hear me:
I am desperate with grief,
I tear my own flesh raw.   90
In this palace of pain
My bed tells a tale of tears
For my father dead.
He did not die nobly in battle,
Feasting with Ares in a foreign land:
My mother, and Aegisthus
Her bedmate, like foresters,
Split his skull with a blood-red axe.

I am the only one to mourn   100

Your death, Agamemnon, father,
Your sharp, cruel death.
To the shimmering stars,
To the light of day,
I shall weep unending tears.
Like the nightingale who killed her child
I shall cry out my grief
Here at my father's gate
For the world to hear.
110 O spirits of Hell,
Powers of the Underworld,
Furies, daughters of the gods,
Look at the husband killed,
The marriage-bed defiled.
Punish them! Avenge his death!
Help me; bring Orestes home.
I am crushed with grief,
A burden of pain
120 Too great to bear alone.

WOMEN.
Electra, child, child of the murderess,
Why pine your life away?
Why this gnawing, endless grief
For him, for Agamemnon?
He was caught in the godless snare
Your witch-mother set for him;
He was cheated in death by a criminal's hand.
I say this: they killed, they must die.

ELECTRA.
Kind friends,
130 You have come to comfort me.
I know, I understand.
But you must let me weep,
Let me mourn my poor father's death.
Oh my dear friends,
I beg you,
Let me weep for him,
Oh, let me weep.

WOMEN.
   He has gone to the shores of Hell,
   The resting-place all mortals come to.
   No tears or prayers will bring him back.
   You are eating your life away   140
   In a grief past bearing.
   There is no help in tears:
   The crime is done, and cannot be cured.
   Is it not time to give up this misery?

ELECTRA.
   Feeble
   A child who will not grieve
   For her father dead.
   I am like the nightingale,
   God's messenger, crying 'Itys! Itys!'
   Forever sorrowing. I am like
   Niobe, all tears,
   A goddess of stone   150
   Weeping, weeping.

WOMEN.
   Electra, my child, you are not alone
   In your tears, alone of humankind.
   You share the grief that racks you so
   With your own sisters, here in the house:
   Chrysothemis, and Iphianassa too.
   And there is another,
   Fretting out his youth in hiding,   160
   Waiting for the happy day
   When Zeus will guide him
   Home to royal Mycenae:
   Orestes, the exile, returned at last.

ELECTRA.
   Orestes! Does he know how I wait for him?
   I have no husband, no children;
   Day after day, uncomforted,
   I bear my burden, weep useless tears.
   Does he know of the crimes committed,
   The wrongs I tell him? Does he care?   170

He says he is longing to be here –
Why does he say so, and never come?

WOMEN.

Electra my child, do not despair.
Lord Zeus is still master in heaven:
He sees, and knows, and rules all things.
Your anger racks you: leave it to him.
You can blunt your fury's edge
And still not forget your father.
Time is a soothing, healing power.
Your brother, Agamemnon's son,
180 In his seaside home by the pastures of Crisa,
Will not forget; and the lord of Hell,
Avenger of the dead, will remember too.

ELECTRA.

The bright flower of my life is withered;
My hope is gone, my strength destroyed.
I have no children to comfort me,
No loving husband to stand by me.
I am no better than a slave,
190 A drudge in my father's halls.
Dressed in these rags
I stand with the other slaves
And feed on the scraps our masters leave.

WOMEN.

There were bitter cries as he came home
From Troy; bitter cries as he took his place
At the table for the feast,
Where a swift sharp axe was waiting.
The witch-wife planned, the lover struck:
Dark powers mingled with mortals
And the deed was done –
200 Foul mating spawned a fouler crime.

ELECTRA.

Bitter that day
More than all other days;
Bitter that night,
That feast unspeakable.

He saw his own death
Glinting in their hands;
Their fingers gripped me,
Twisted and broke my life.
O Zeus, lord of Olympus,
Punish them with pain,   210
Deal dreadful death,
Turn triumph to dust.

WOMEN.
    You have said enough, Electra.
    Can you not see that what you do,
    What you say, will bring you more pain,
    Worse suffering still?
    You are sullen and stubborn,
    Breeding endless arguments,
    A treasury of grief.
    If you fight with power, you'll lose.   220

ELECTRA.
    I have no choice.
    I am on the rack.
    My stubbornness is born of pain.
    Till my dying breath
    I shall feed on his hate.
    What words can comfort me?
    O my dear friends,
    There are no words.
    Leave me, leave me:
    I am sick, past cure,
    Walking a long road   230
    Of endless misery.

FIRST WOMAN.
    Electra, listen to me.
    Trust me. I speak
    As a mother to her child.
    Do not make bad worse.

ELECTRA.
    Is there an end to unhappiness?
    How is it right to forget the dead?

It's unheard-of: I won't do it.
240 Even if I lived a life of ease,
Content, I should never clip
The wings of mourning for my father.
If the dead are dust
And nothingness, no more;
If murderers live
Free of the price of blood,
How can we say
That respect and shame
250 Still exist in the world of mortals

FIRST WOMAN.

Child, whether you follow our advice
Or not, you'll always find us loyal friends.
Your good is our good, now and forever.

ELECTRA.

Dear friends, you must forgive me if I seem
Forever complaining, weeping endless tears.
My life compels it. What else can I do?
What woman of birth, of spirit, would suffer
As I have suffered, and say nothing?
My father, dead. Injustice, flowering
260 Unchecked. Day and night, an agony of grief.
My own mother, who gave me birth,
Hated, hated. My father's palace, shared
With his murderers. The King! The Queen!
I'm theirs: they allow me life, or death.

Think what it means to see, day after day,
Aegisthus sitting on my father's throne,
Wearing my father's robes. Day after day
I watch him pouring libations to the gods
270 There at the hearth where he butchered him.
And hardest of all to bear, night after night
I see them together in my father's bed:
The murderer and her — shall I call her
My unhappy mother, or Aegisthus' whore? —
That shameless one, who sleeps with a criminal,
Fearing no Fury; she laughs at what she did,

And makes the day a festival – the day
She tricked my father and murdered him,
The day she celebrates each month with hymns
And offerings to the 'gods who saved the state'.   280
All this I must watch – here in the palace –
Weeping in misery, mourning alone
At the feast named for my father's death.
When I weep, I weep in secret – this is
No grief to be indulged in public tears.
Even so, the woman they call Her Majesty
Comes up to me and scolds me, saying,
'Cursed of the gods! Are you the only one
To lose a father, the only one on earth
Ever to mourn? Damn you! May the gods   290
Of the Underworld give you good cause to weep!'

These insults are enough – except when she hears
Rumours that Orestes is coming home.
Then she is wild with fury, stands over me
And screams, 'It's you I have to thank for this!
You did it! You snatched him from my hands
And stole him to safety. You rescued him,
And soon enough you'll pay the penalty!'
So the bitch-mother yaps; and by her side
Her noble bridegroom stands and nods –
Aegisthus, the toothless lion, plague of our state,   300
The woman-at-arms she nerves to fight.

One day, Orestes will come home and end it.
The waiting has wasted my life with grief.
'He's coming soon,' they said once.
And still they say he's coming. My hope is dead.
O my dear friends, you see how I suffer.
Tell me, why should I hold back my tears?
Why should I show honour or respect?
In a dark world my path is darkness too.

FIRST WOMAN.   310
    Where is Aegisthus? These are wild words.
    Is he here in Argos or away from home?

ELECTRA.
>He's away, on his country estates.
>If he'd been here I would have stayed indoors.

FIRST WOMAN.
>In that case . . . if he's away . . . then perhaps
>This is the time to ask . . . if you can say . . .

ELECTRA.
>He's away. Ask what you want to know.

FIRST WOMAN.
>Orestes your brother . . . can you tell us,
>Is he on his way? Is he coming home?

ELECTRA.
>We have his promise. We have nothing more.

FIRST WOMAN.
320 The task is fearful. All men would hesitate.

ELECTRA.
>I did not hesitate to save his life.

FIRST WOMAN.
>The prince will come and save the ones he loves.

ELECTRA.
>I trust him, or I'd not have lived so long.

FIRST WOMAN.
>Say no more now. Look: your sister Chrysothemis,
>Your dear sister, is coming from the palace.
>She brings funeral-gifts,
>Tomb-offerings to pay the dead below.

>   *Enter* CHRYSOTHEMIS.

CHRYSOTHEMIS.
>Electra, indoors is the place for women.
>You know that. Why do you come out here,
330 Where all Argos is listening? Will you never learn?
>What good does all your empty anger do?
>I feel what has happened, too –
>I feel it bitterly. If only I dared,

If only I had the strength, I'd show my hate.
But I prefer to bend before the storm;
I'll never threaten what I cannot do.
If this is cowardice, you be a coward too!
I know that you are right and I am wrong –
But I must be free, I can never be a slave:
And to be free, I must bow to the king and queen.   340

ELECTRA.
It's hard to believe. You are Chrysothemis,
Agamemnon's daughter – and still you place
Your mother first. The advice you offer me
Is hers, not yours. She told you the words to use.
You'll have to choose, Chrysothemis, choose now:
Will you defy her – like a fool, like me –
Or obey her, and betray the ones you love?
You say if you dared, if you had the strength,
You'd show how much you hate them. Well, then:
I am working to avenge our father –
Will you refuse to help? Will you discourage me?   350
Must we add cowardice to suffering?

You advise me to accept, to give up my grief.
What good would that do? I have my life:
A life of misery, but I chose it
And I am satisfied. I give them pain,
A grave-gift to make my father smile,
If the dead below can smile. You hate them,
Or so you tell me. But your hate is words,
Not deeds. In all you do, you honour them.   360

You say I must bow to the king and queen.
Will they reward me with the gifts you love –
Groaning tables, a life of ease? Keep them!
I feast on peace of mind –
A banquet you'd choose yourself, if you were wise.
People could call you Agamemnon's daughter,
Child of the noblest man who ever lived;
Instead, they call you Clytemnestra's child,
Who betrayed her father and everyone she loved.

FIRST WOMAN.
  My dears, no good will come of quarrelling.
370 Listen to each other: listen and learn.

CHRYSOTHEMIS.
  I'm used to the way she speaks to me.
  I'd never have begun this argument
  Except for my dreadful news. Disaster
  Is coming, to stop her complaints forever.

ELECTRA.
  Disaster? What disaster? Tell me.
  What could be worse than what I suffer now?

CHRYSOTHEMIS.
  Listen: this is what I overheard.
  You must stop these complaints, or else
  They'll have you taken away from here
  And walled up forever in a living grave.
380 You'll never see daylight again;
  You'll cry your cries, and no one will hear.
  Electra, listen to me! Give way now!
  Or else, when the blow has fallen, don't blame me.

ELECTRA.
  Is that what they plan to do to me?

CHRYSOTHEMIS.
  When Aegisthus comes home, exactly that.

ELECTRA.
  If that's all, may the gods send him quickly home.

CHRYSOTHEMIS.
  What do you mean? What kind of prayer is that?

ELECTRA.
  A prayer to the gods to send Aegisthus home.

CHRYSOTHEMIS.
390 Are you such a fool? The sooner he comes –

ELECTRA.
  The sooner he comes, the sooner I'll escape.

CHRYSOTHEMIS.
  Are you so eager to give up your life?

ELECTRA.
  A fine life, a life to wonder at!

CHRYSOTHEMIS.
  It would be if you chose to make it so.

ELECTRA.
  You mean if I betrayed the ones I love.

CHRYSOTHEMIS.
  All I mean is this. Bow to the king and queen.

ELECTRA.
  You bow! You grovel! That's not my way.

CHRYSOTHEMIS.
  You're mad, and your madness will destroy you.

ELECTRA.
  Destroy me or not, I shall avenge him first.

CHRYSOTHEMIS.
  He'll not blame me. He understands, I know.   400

ELECTRA.
  A coward's thought. Hug it for comfort!

CHRYSOTHEMIS.
  Electra, listen! Follow my advice.

ELECTRA.
  Your advice – and give up what sense I have?

CHRYSOTHEMIS.
  There's no more to say. I must go now.

ELECTRA.
  Where must you go? What offerings are those?

CHRYSOTHEMIS.
  Our mother's, sent for our father's grave.

ELECTRA.
  Offerings – from her? To the man she hated?

CHRYSOTHEMIS.
To the man she killed. Say what you mean.

ELECTRA.
Who persuaded her to make him offerings?

CHRYSOTHEMIS.
410   I think she was sent a warning, in a dream.

ELECTRA.
O gods of Argos, come down to me now!

CHRYSOTHEMIS.
You mean this dream, this warning, gives you hope?

ELECTRA.
Tell me the dream, and I'll know for sure.

CHRYSOTHEMIS.
I know no details. There's little to tell.

ELECTRA.
Tell me what there is. A single word
Can be the word of fate, for good or ill.

CHRYSOTHEMIS.
This is all I know. Our father came:
She saw him in front of her, restored to life.
420   He took the staff of the kings of Argos,
That once was his, and now Aegisthus holds,
And planted it in the earth beside the hearth.
At once it grew and blossomed, a green tree
Whose branches overshadowed all Mycenae.
That was the dream; I heard it from a slave
Who was by her side when she told it
At the altar of Helios, god of the sun.
No more than that: she was terrified,
And gave me these offerings for Agamemnon's grave.
Electra, I beg of you, listen! Don't destroy
430   Yourself. Don't drive me away. Do as I say!

ELECTRA.
Chrysothemis – sister – these offerings:
Make none of them. The gods will not allow

Gifts from that witch-wife to touch our father's grave.
He's sleeping: scatter them on the breeze,
Or bury them deep. They must not reach him.
When she dies, she'll find them waiting,
Mementoes of what she did. I tell you,
She's the most shameless woman left alive,
To send garlands of hate to the man she killed!   440
Does she imagine the corpse will smile his thanks,
His gratitude – to the enemy who killed him?
She butchered him: hacked at his lifeless corpse
And wiped the sword-blade clean in his own hair –
Is her guilt to be wiped away so easily
By these grave-gifts? Do you think that?
No! Throw them away. Instead, offer him
A lock of your hair. And give him these gifts
From me: poor gifts, but they are all I have.   450
A twist of hair – dull, not glossy like yours –
And this plain cloth belt. Go down on your knees
And beg him to rise from the grave
And help us. Beg him to bring Orestes home,
A strong arm, a foot to trample our enemies.
When we've won, we'll garland the grave
With richer gifts than any we give him now.

Do you understand, Chrysothemis? I think
Our father sent the dream that frightened her.   460
But even if he did not, do as I ask:
Do it for my sake, for yours, and for his –
Our father, who lies with the dead below.

FIRST WOMAN.
My child, do as she asks. She speaks
With a daughter's love. Help her, do as she asks.

CHRYSOTHEMIS.
Yes. I'll do it, and do it at once.
My duty is clear, and needs no arguing.
Only . . . if you are my friends, I beg you
By all the gods, help me, keep it secret:
If our mother finds out what I have done,   470
What I have dared, my tears will be the price.

Exit CHRYSOTHEMIS.

WOMEN.
> Am I wise? Do I understand?
> Was this an omen, sent
> By Justice the Avenger?
> Soon, my child,
> She will come down to us
> And bring the strength we need.
> When we heard that dream
480 > A breeze of hope
> Stirred in our hearts.
> Your father, warlord of the Greeks,
> Has not abandoned you;
> The axe, the double axe,
> The butcher's bronze
> Which showed no mercy then
> Will show none now.

> The avenging Furies hide,
490 > Waiting to pounce –
> They are an army
> Marching in bronze;
> They are monsters of doom
> Who sniff the murderers out,
> The lecherous, unlawful lust,
> The butchers, coupling in blood.
> A breeze of hope
> Stirs in our hearts.
> Was Agamemnon's ghost
> Glimpsed in the night
500 > A true omen? If not,
> All dreams, all prophecies,
> Wither and die.

> For the house of Pelops
> A chariot-race long ago
> Began the line of death.
> The prize was marriage,
> The king's own daughter's hand;
> And Pelops won the race.

For Myrtilus, who challenged him,
Disaster came, and death.
Hurled headlong from the golden car,   510
Cheated and tricked,
He drowned in the roaring sea:
An evil omen
For Pelops and all his line.
Now misery and death
Still haunt this house.

   Enter CLYTEMNESTRA.

CLYTEMNESTRA.
  Still you go freely, anywhere you choose!
  If Aegisthus were here, he'd keep you
  Indoors, where you'd bring us no disgrace.
  But he's away, and you pay no heed to me,
  Although you cry to the whole world
  That I'm a tyrant, crushing you alive.
  How am I harming you? With these hard words?
  They are no harder than your words to me.   520

  You talk of nothing but your father.
  You say I caused his death – and I admit it.
  What you say is true. I caused his death –
  In Justice's name. The criminal paid –
  In Justice's name. I helped – as you
  Should have helped – in Justice's name.
  This father of yours, the father you mourn,   530
  Did what no other Greek has ever dared:
  He took his own daughter, Iphigenia,
  Your sister, and sacrificed her to the gods.
  His own child! Her begetting caused him no pain,
  Compared to mine when I gave her birth.
  Why should he kill her? For the Greeks?
  They had no right to take a child of mine.
  For his brother Menelaus' sake?
  If that was his excuse, he deserved his death.
  Menelaus had two children of his own –
  They should have died before my daughter.   540
  Their father and mother began the Trojan War.

Was it some hunger of the king of Hades,
Greed for my daughter's flesh, not theirs?
The children of Menelaus! Were they
The only ones your father ever loved?

He was callous and cruel, a murderer.
How can you deny it? Your own sister
Iphigenia would say so, if the dead could speak.
I caused his death, Electra – and I'm glad,
550 Not sorry. Before you call me a criminal,
Consider who is right and who is wrong.

ELECTRA.

I've said nothing, this time,
To deserve such angry words.
Will you let me answer, let me say what must
Be said, for my father's and sister's sake?

CLYTEMNESTRA.

Speak. It's allowed. If you always began
With such respect, I'd be glad to hear.

ELECTRA.

I have this to say. You admit that you killed
My father. Just or unjust, right or wrong,
560 That was a monstrous crime. And I say
That it was wrong: you were snared by Aegisthus' charms.
That criminal! The man you bed with now!
Ask the hunting-goddess, ask Artemis,
What sin made her hold back the winds
At Aulis. No, I will tell you:
No mortal must question a god.
This is the story. Agamemnon was hunting
In her sacred wood; his footsteps startled
A dappled, antlered stag – her sacred stag.
He took aim, and killed it. The stag's death
570 And the hunter's triumph angered Artemis.
She held back the wind, becalmed the fleet.
The price for the deer, the price she set
For a wind, was Agamemnon's daughter's life.
Only that sacrifice would unlock the fleet
And give them fair sailing, for home or Troy.

He did no favour for Menelaus.
He was forced to kill her. He had no choice.

But even if it had been a favour, even if
You were right, and he murdered his own child
To gratify his brother – would that give you
The right to murder him? Blood for blood –
Is that your law? If so, you condemn yourself: 580
You killed; now you must die.

But you're wrong. These are empty words.
Do they explain the worst sin of all?
You sleep with a murderer, the man
Who helped you kill my father;
You sleep with him, and make new children
To take the place of those you have driven out.
What excuse can you give for that?   590
Is it revenge for Iphigenia's death –
Was this monstrous marriage made to avenge her
    death?
Is that what you say? Is that what you call just?

You refuse to listen to me;
You scream that I'm insolent,
Impertinent to my mother. Mother!
Jailer, I call you. I live
No better than a slave; I'm heaped
With insults by you and your . . . bedmate.   600
And Orestes too, Orestes who escaped you,
Is fretting away his life in exile.
You blame me for that: you say
I saved him to punish you one day.
If only I had! If only I could!
Call me what names you like: wild,
Shameless, impertinent. My answer is
That it's true. I am all of them:
My mother's true daughter in every way.

FIRST WOMAN.
    She's furious – too furious to care   610
    Whether what she says is right or wrong.

CLYTEMNESTRA.
> But I care. She's not a child.
> You hear the way she speaks
> To her own mother. Is there more to come?
> Fresh insolence? Is she not ashamed?

ELECTRA.
> Ashamed? Of course I'm ashamed,
> Whatever you choose to think. Remember:
> If I go too far, if I forget myself,
> The fault is yours. Your treatment
> 620   Forces me to answer hate with hate.
> Evil breeds evil – I learned from you.

CLYTEMNESTRA.
> That's enough! Such insolence! You talk
> Too much of what I do and what I say.

ELECTRA.
> No! Your own words, your own actions,
> Speak for themselves. They need no words from me.

CLYTEMNESTRA.
> Artemis, queen of heaven! When Aegisthus
> Comes home, you'll suffer for this.

ELECTRA.
> You see? You allow me to speak, and then
> You lose your temper and refuse to hear.

CLYTEMNESTRA.
> 630   I've heard enough, allowed enough!
> Now hold your tongue, and let me sacrifice.

ELECTRA.
> Go! Sacrifice! I'll hold my tongue.
> I've said my say: there is nothing more.

CLYTEMNESTRA.
> Slave, bring forward the offerings.
> I'll pray now; I'll ask
> Lord Apollo to free me from these fears.
> Apollo! Protector! Hear and answer
> The prayers I speak, and the secret prayers

Locked in my heart. I dare not
Unveil my thoughts while she is here,
My enemy, standing beside me,   640
A malicious tongue, eager as ever
For gossip to scatter in the town.
Hear my words, and hear my hidden thoughts.

Lycean Apollo, I dreamed of a ghost
In the night, a vision with no clear meaning.
If the omen is good, fulfil it;
If it's bad, turn it aside,
Turn it against my enemies.
They are plotting to hurl me down
From the rich seat of power. Prevent them!
Grant me forever unbroken peace,   650
Unbroken power in the house of Atreus.
Let me live a life of love with those
Who love me, with all of my children
Whose minds are not sick with bitter hate.

Hear me, Apollo! Grant these prayers,
For mine and the city's sake. Fulfil
The words I speak, the wishes of my heart.
You understand my secret prayers,
For nothing is hidden from the son of Zeus.

Enter the SERVANT.

SERVANT.
Ladies . . . I wonder, can you tell me   660
If this is the palace of Lord Aegisthus?

FIRST WOMAN.
Yes, sir. You have found it. This is the place.

SERVANT.
And that royal lady . . . there by the altar . . .
Is that Clytemnestra? Is that the queen?

FIRST WOMAN.
You are in the presence of the queen herself.

SERVANT.
Your Majesty, I come from friends, with news –
Good news, for Lord Aegisthus and yourself.

CLYTEMNESTRA.
An omen from heaven! I welcome it.
What news, sir? Where are you from?

SERVANT.
670   I was sent by Phanoteus of Phocis.

CLYTEMNESTRA.
An old friend. You bring good news
From a good friend. What is it? Speak.

SERVANT.
Orestes is dead. Just that, no more.

ELECTRA.
O gods! Orestes – ? How can I bear it?

CLYTEMNESTRA.
Again! Again! Ignore her. Tell me again.

SERVANT.
He's dead, my lady. Orestes is dead.

ELECTRA.
O Zeus! Will you not kill me too?

CLYTEMNESTRA.
Be quiet. Leave us in peace. And you, sir,
Tell me in detail, exactly how he died.

SERVANT.
680   Yes, my lady. It was for that I was sent.
Orestes had gone to the Pythian Games
In Delphi, the best in Greece. The Games began,
And heralds announced the opening event:
A footrace. Orestes stood up to take part,
A dazzling figure, admired by everyone.
He ran the race; his performance matched
His appearance; he won the victor's crown.

After that, what can I say? To cut it short,

No other competitor could match him.
Whatever competition was announced –   690
Sprinting, distance, pentathlon – he won with ease,
And stood smiling while the victor's name was called:
'Orestes, son of Agamemnon, son
Of the general who once commanded Greece.'

So far, so good. But when a god sends harm,
What mortal can escape, however fine and strong?
The day for the chariot-race arrived.
It was a fast event, and began at dawn.
Ten competitors moved to the starting-line: 700
An Achaean, a Spartan, and next to them
Two drivers from Cyrene, skilful and fast.
Orestes was fifth in line, driving a team
Of mares from Thessaly; an Aetolian sixth,
With chestnut colts; a Magnesian seventh;
The eighth, an Aenian, was driving bays;
The ninth was from Athens, founded by the gods,
And a Boeotian, tenth, completed the line.

So they waited in line, each chariot
Keeping well inside its allotted place.   710
The trumpet blared, and they were off. Each man
Shouted to his horses, and shook the reins;
The pounding of hooves and rattle of chariots
Filled all the course; dust billowed to the sky.

For the first few laps they were tightly bunched.
There was no mercy: they goaded their horses on.
Each driver tried to inch his chariot past
His opponent's wheels, his opponent's team.
The horses were snorting foam; flecked with its drops   720
They hurtled on, neck and neck, wheel by flying wheel.

To begin with, none of them overturned.
Then, suddenly, on the turn from the sixth
To the seventh laps, the Aenian's horses took
The bit between their teeth; they swerved across
The course, head-on into one of the teams
From Cyrene. After that, crash followed crash

As driver after driver bit the dust.
730   The course was a battlefield, choked with wrecks.

The Athenian driver, an old hand,
Had seen this danger coming. He drew in
And let the sea of hooves and wheels go by,
Surging up the centre of the track. Orestes
Had stayed behind him, keeping his mares fresh
For a victory-gallop in the final lap.
When he saw that only the Athenian
Was left to beat, he shouted to his team
And gave chase. Neck and neck they pounded on;
740   First one, then the other, inched ahead.

Orestes was on the inside. Each time he passed
The turning-post at the end of the lap,
His axle almost grazed it; just in time, each time,
He pulled to the right, and gave his horses rein.
He made the turn each time, with no damage
To himself or his chariot. So far, so good.
But then, on the last lap, he misjudged the turn,
Slipped rein too soon, and hit the turning-post.
The axle splintered, and Orestes was hurled
Across the driver's handrail to the ground.
He was tangled in broken reins; his horses
Bolted, and dragged him feet first across the course.

750   The crowd groaned in sympathy to see him fall –
So many triumphs, such a dreadful end.
He was smashed on the ground, tossed headlong
In the air. At last, after a struggle, grooms
Managed to control the runaways, and cut
His mangled body free: torn, oozing blood,
Hard even for his friends to recognise.

They burned the corpse at once, on a funeral pyre.
And now a burial-party is coming here
760   From Phocis, bringing his ashes – so great
A man, poor ashes in a little urn! –
To be laid to rest in his native land.

Your Majesty, that is my story – sad

To hear, but for those of us who saw it
The worst disaster our eyes have ever seen.

FIRST WOMAN.
The last shoot of the royal house, destroyed!
The dynasty of Argos has withered and died.

CLYTEMNESTRA.
O Zeus! Is this the news I longed to hear,
The pain that sets me free? Can I be glad
To be safe at last, by my own son's death?

SERVANT.
My lady, why does this news distress you so?

CLYTEMNESTRA.
I was his mother. However she is wronged,   770
A mother never hates the child she bore.

SERVANT.
Then I was wrong to tell you, wrong to come?

CLYTEMNESTRA.
Wrong? No. How could it be wrong to bring me proof,
Clear proof that he is dead? He was my own son,
Flesh of my flesh. He tore himself away
From his own mother's milk; he went into exile,
A stranger, far from home. From that day on
He held me guilty of Agamemnon's death;
He swore vengeance; he snatched my sleep away;
Night and day, I knew I was marked for death.   780

And now, today, you tell me he is dead.
I am free of fear at last: fear of my son,
And fear of that thirsty one who lives with me,
Drinking my life. Now her brother is dead,
I can ignore her threats. I can live in peace.

ELECTRA.
O Orestes, my poor Orestes!
To die as you died, and now to be mocked
By your own mother! How you are suffering!   790

CLYTEMNESTRA.
No: you are suffering. His sufferings are done.

ELECTRA.
Avenging Furies, do you hear her now?

CLYTEMNESTRA.
They heard me then: heard me and judged the case.

ELECTRA.
Yes, gloat! Insult us! Enjoy your victory!

CLYTEMNESTRA.
You'll not stop me, then – either of you?

ELECTRA.
We have been stopped. We can't stop you now.

CLYTEMNESTRA.
Do you hear that, my friend? Your journey here
Deserves a rich reward: you've stopped her tongue.

SERVANT.
There's no more to say. May I go now?

CLYTEMNESTRA.
800   Go now? Before I show my gratitude
To yourself and my good friend who sent you here?
Come inside. Leave her out here, squealing
Her sorrows, and the fate of those she loved.

    Exeunt SERVANT *and* CLYTEMNESTRA.

ELECTRA.
Did you see how she suffered? Did you see
Her agonies of grief for the son she lost?
She laughed, and left. O Orestes, Orestes,
My darling, your death is my death too.
810   You have torn from my heart the last rags of hope –
That you would come home, to punish them
For my father's death and what they have done to me.
Where must I turn now? I have no one:
He is dead, and you are dead. Must I go inside
And bow to them again, the masters I hate,
My father's butchers? Must I suffer that?

I'll never go in again. I'll lie down,
Here at the gate, and starve to death, alone.

And if they see me, if they are angry,   820
Let them kill me – for charity, kill me now.
What use is my life to me? It is agony.

WOMEN.
Where are Zeus' thunderbolts?
Where is the fiery Sun?
Are they sleeping? Why
Do they not scorch this guilt?

ELECTRA.
Ah . . . ah . . .

FIRST WOMAN.
My poor child . . .

ELECTRA.
No . . . no . . .

FIRST WOMAN.
Don't cry. Hush, child.
No more weeping.   830

ELECTRA.
You are breaking my heart.

FIRST WOMAN.
How?

ELECTRA.
They are in Hades; they have gone
Down to the underworld forever.
Will you still offer me hope?
Leave me. Leave me to weep.

FIRST WOMAN.
There was a King, Amphiaraus:
Snared by a woman
For a necklace of gold;
And now, in the underworld . . .

ELECTRA.
Ah . . . ah . . .   840

FIRST WOMAN.
He rules among the dead.

ELECTRA.
  No . . . no . . .

FIRST WOMAN.
  And the woman,
  The murderess . . .

ELECTRA.
  Paid with her life?

FIRST WOMAN.
  Yes.

ELECTRA.
  Yes! A champion rose up
  To avenge his death.
  Where is my champion?
  He is snatched away and gone.

FIRST WOMAN.
  Your life is cruel and hard.

ELECTRA.
850 I have borne all there is to bear.
  Whirlpools of grief,
  Unending misery.

FIRST WOMAN.
  We have seen your suffering.

ELECTRA.
  Leave me to suffer, then.
  Do not flatter me –

FIRST WOMAN.
  How?

ELECTRA.
  By offering empty hope:
860 My brother, my royal father's son.

FIRST WOMAN.
  All men must die one day.

ELECTRA.
  Like him? Like poor Orestes?

In a tangle of reins,
A trampling of hooves?

FIRST WOMAN.
A bitter sight to see.

ELECTRA.
A bitter death. Far
From home, far away –

FIRST WOMAN.
Far . . .

ELECTRA.
In a stranger's grave
Unwept, unmourned. 870

Enter CHRYSOTHEMIS.

CHRYSOTHEMIS.
Electra! My dear, darling Electra!
I picked up my skirts, and ran all the way
To tell you. Wonderful news! The end
Of all your suffering, the end of your grief!

ELECTRA.
My grief, and suffering, are past all cure.
No news is wonderful. No news can help.

CHRYSOTHEMIS.
Orestes is here! He has come back to us!
I know it, as sure as I am standing here.

ELECTRA.
You're babbling. How can you be so cruel?
Must you laugh at your own unhappiness, and 880
  mine?

CHRYSOTHEMIS.
I swear by the gods of Argos, it's true.
This is no mockery. Orestes is back.

ELECTRA.
No. You're wrong. What made you think so?
Has someone told you this, persuaded you?

CHRYSOTHEMIS.
  I know it for myself, from no one else.
  I saw clear proof: I saw, with my own eyes.

ELECTRA.
  What proof did you see? You're on fire,
  Blazing with hope. What proof did you see?

CHRYSOTHEMIS.
  Just listen, Electra! Then, when I've done,
890 See if you still think I'm babbling. Listen!

ELECTRA.
  Tell me, then, if telling brings you joy.

CHRYSOTHEMIS.
  This is what happened. When I went just now
  To take the offerings to our father's grave,
  I saw that the top of the mound was wet
  With a grave-gift of milk, and there were flowers,
  All kinds of flowers, round it in wreaths.
  I stood there amazed. I looked all round,
  In case anyone was near. But the whole place
  Was deserted and still. I crept nearer,
900 Up to the grave. There, lying on the edge,
  There was another offering: a lock
  Of hair, newly cut off. As soon as I saw it,
  My whole being filled with thoughts of him:
  Orestes our brother, dearest of men.
  I picked it up; I could say nothing;
  My eyes were blurred with tears. I know,
  Electra, I know now as I knew then,
  That Orestes is here. These offerings
  Are his, they can have come from no one else.
  Only you or I ever visit the grave.
910 I did not leave them. You could not have gone:
  If you leave the palace yard, even to pray,
  They punish you. Was it our mother? No!
  Why should she choose to go? And even if
  She had, she would have said, we would have known.

  No. They can have come only from Orestes.

Take heart, Electra! Our luck must change.
Until now, sorrow and pain; but from today
Unending joy, unending happiness!

ELECTRA.
Fool! Do you know nothing? I pity you.   920

CHRYSOTHEMIS.
What is it? Does what I say not please you?

ELECTRA.
You know nothing. You're in a world of dreams.

CHRYSOTHEMIS.
What more should I know? I know what I saw!

ELECTRA.
You fool, he's dead. Orestes is dead.
He can do nothing to help us. Forget him.

CHRYSOTHEMIS.
How do you know? Who told you he was dead?

ELECTRA.
A man who was there, who saw him die.

CHRYSOTHEMIS.
I don't believe it. Where is he now?   930

ELECTRA.
In the palace – our mother's welcome guest.

CHRYSOTHEMIS.
But if he is dead – Orestes – who left
The offerings? Who visited the grave?

ELECTRA.
A stranger, perhaps: a pious stranger
Who left them to honour Orestes' death.

CHRYSOTHEMIS.
To think I ran to bring you such good news!
How could I know, how could I understand
This new burden of grief, new misery
To add to the old? Electra, how could I know?

ELECTRA.
You understand at last. Now, listen to me.
There's still a way for you to ease our grief.

CHRYSOTHEMIS.
940 How can there be? Must I bring the dead to life?

ELECTRA.
It's foolish to think so. There are other ways.

CHRYSOTHEMIS.
If only I have the strength. What must I do?

ELECTRA.
Be brave, and do exactly as I say.

CHRYSOTHEMIS.
If I can help, I'll do what I can.

ELECTRA.
Remember, to win we must be prepared to fight.

CHRYSOTHEMIS.
I understand. I'll not refuse to help.

ELECTRA.
Listen, then. These are my hopes, my plans.
First, you must realise we are alone –
Our dear ones have been snatched by the lord of death,
950 And only we are left. There is no one else.
While Orestes was alive, and safe, I had hopes
That one day he would come back to Argos
And punish the murderers. But he is dead,
And I must turn to you, Chrysothemis.
Will you help your sister? Will you nerve yourself
To butcher that butcher, that criminal,
Aegisthus? There. Nothing is hidden now.

Think. Will you help me, or do nothing still?
What else can you cling to? Your hope is dead.
960 Only grief is left, grief that you have lost
A noble father, a rich inheritance,
Grief that your life is withering away
With no husband, no children and no hope.

Yes! You can put away all marriage-thoughts –
Unless you think Aegisthus such a fool
That he would let a child of yours or mine
Be born, grow up and live – to murder him.

All your hope is in me, Chrysothemis.
If you help me, if you do as I ask,
You will be honoured by the dead below –
Our father, our brother. You will be free,   970
No longer a slave; you will be a child
Worthy of Agamemnon; a prince's bride.

Help me, and these are the names you will win.
The citizens of Argos, and strangers too,
Will greet us with honour. 'Look,' they will say,
'There go the sisters who saved the royal house;
They turned on a triumphant enemy
And cut him down; they avenged their father's death.
They strut like heroes – men, not women: 980
Sing them hymns of praise, and celebrate
Their bravery, the glory of their name.'

Our courage will be known over all the world.
Alive or dead, we'll be remembered, always.
Do as I ask, Chrysothemis! Be brave
And fight, for our father's and brother's sake.
Leave cowardice to cowards! Arm yourself
To end our weakness, our suffering, for evermore.

FIRST WOMAN.
    My children, it's time for caution.   990
    Speak well; listen well. Do nothing rash.

CHRYSOTHEMIS.
    Caution? My friends, she's out of her mind.
    You heard what she intends to do; you heard
    Her ask me to help. Where is caution in that?

    You have no power, Electra. Your only weapon
    Is rashness. How can I help? How can you hope
    To win? You're a woman, not a man.
    You're weak, and your enemies are strong.
    The gods favour them; their strength grows day by day;

Ours withers and shrinks away. Kings in their power!
1000 If you challenge them, you'll destroy yourself.
When Aegisthus gets to hear these plans of yours,
He'll punish us both, with punishments
Worse than all we suffer now. You say
We'll win glory and honour. What good is that
If we die like criminals – or worse than that,
1010 If they make us live, if they'll not let us die?

Give up your anger. You're destroying us.
The last survivors of the royal house –
Must we die too? I beg you, Electra,
Give up your anger. The words you said
Can be unsaid, forgotten – I'll see to that.
But you must give way; you must realise
At last that you are weak and they are strong.
Admit it! Bow to the king and queen!

FIRST WOMAN.
 My child, do as she says. The greatest gifts
 In human life are caution and common sense.

ELECTRA.
 You say nothing unexpected. I knew
 You'd refuse: there was no need to ask.
 It's there, it must be done. I must do it.
1020 If no one will help, I must do it alone.

CHRYSOTHEMIS.
 And what of the day they killed our father –
 And you did nothing? Where was your courage then?

ELECTRA.
 How could I kill them then? I was too yong.

CHRYSOTHEMIS.
 If you were too young then, be too young now!

ELECTRA.
 There's no more to say. You refuse to help.

CHRYSOTHEMIS.
 You'll destroy yourself. Of course I refuse.

ELECTRA.
Wise coward! I admire you, and despise you too.

CHRYSOTHEMIS.
One day you'll admit I was right. Till then –

ELECTRA.
Till *then*? A day that will never come!

CHRYSOTHEMIS.
No one can tell the future. We shall see.   1030

ELECTRA.
Go inside. I have finished now.

CHRYSOTHEMIS.
If only you'd listen! If only you'd –

ELECTRA.
Go inside. Tell your mother all you've heard.

CHRYSOTHEMIS.
Electra! How can you think I hate you so?

ELECTRA.
You despise me. You want me to give way.

CHRYSOTHEMIS.
I want to save you. Is that despising you?

ELECTRA.
And to be saved, I must do what you call right?

CHRYSOTHEMIS.
It is right. Do it, and then I can help.

ELECTRA.
You're so clever! So clever – and so wrong.

CHRYSOTHEMIS.
It's you that's wrong. Why can't you understand?   1040

ELECTRA.
How is it wrong to fight for what is right?

CHRYSOTHEMIS.
If you destroy yourself, then it is wrong.

ELECTRA.
Your principle, not mine.

CHRYSOTHEMIS.
If you attack the king, you'll see I was right.

ELECTRA.
Whatever you say, I *shall* attack the king.

CHRYSOTHEMIS.
Will nothing stop you? Will nothing change your mind?

ELECTRA.
Change right for wrong? Courage for cowardice? No!

CHRYSOTHEMIS.
You refuse to listen, whatever I say?

ELECTRA.
I've made up my mind; I'll never change.

CHRYSOTHEMIS.
There's no more to say. You refuse to see
1050 That all I ask is common sense;
I'll never agree that what you are doing is right.

ELECTRA.
Go inside. We are walking separate paths.
However much you try, you'll not persuade me:
You're chasing shadows – a foolish task.

CHRYSOTHEMIS.
Go on, then, if you think yourself so wise.
But when you've tried and failed, when you suffer,
You'll remember my words and agree at last.

  Exit CHRYSOTHEMIS.

WOMEN.
Look up, and see: birds of the air,
1060 With tender devotion, protect and cherish
The adults who gave them life,
Who reared them. Why are we not the same?
Have we not the same debt to pay?
In the name of the thunderbolt of Zeus,

In the name of Justice, enthroned on high,
Where there is crime, there must be punishment.
O voice of the listening Dead,
Cry sorrow to them now,
The children of Atreus under the earth:
Cry bitterness and shame.

Tell them the sickness of the house;   1070
Tell them of two sisters, once loving friends,
Now twisted enemies: all love,
All charity forgotten. Tell them, too,
How Electra is sailing the storm alone,
Weeping still for a father lost –
Like a nightingale: crying, crying . . .
Loyal Electra! How gladly
She would die, how gladly
She would leave the light of day,
If only she could snatch away
The twin monsters of the house.   1080

Nobility of soul will never stoop
To live as cowards live,
Tarnished, dishonoured.
O my child, my child,
You have chosen this path,
The common path of grief.
You are armed against evil;
You are called loyal, and wise.

O gods, may we live to see   1090
Agamemnon's daughter
Triumph against the enemies
Who trample her now!
Electra, child of misery,
You have honoured the laws
Of the gods, you have honoured Zeus:
You will destroy your enemies.

Enter ORESTES *and* PYLADES, PYLADES *carrying an
urn.*

ORESTES.
> Ladies, I wonder . . . is this the place
> We are looking for? Have we taken the right road?

FIRST WOMAN.
1100   What place, sir? Have you some business here?

ORESTES.
> I'm looking for King Aegisthus' house.

FIRST WOMAN.
> This is it. You've taken the right road.

ORESTES.
> Thank you. I wonder, would one of you go inside
> And tell him we bring him longed-for news?

FIRST WOMAN.
> She'll do it. She's closest to them in blood.

ORESTES.
> Woman, go inside, if you will, and tell them
> That we are here come from Phocis to bring them news.

ELECTRA.
> O Zeus! Zeus! Is this the proof at last?
> Clear proof that the story we heard was true?

ORESTES.
1110   I know nothing of stories. Strophios
> Of Phocis sent me. It's about Orestes.

ELECTRA.
> Orestes? What? I tremble with fear.

ORESTES.
> He's dead, lady. We've brought him home,
> All that's left of him, in a little urn.

ELECTRA.
> How can I bear it? The story was true . . .
> A burden of grief. You have brought him home.

ORESTES.
> If you're weeping for Orestes, he's here:
> His ashes are all that's left, here in this urn.

ELECTRA.

    His ashes . . . here in this urn . . . all that is left.
    Please let me hold it . . . in god's name . . .   1120
    I beg you, on my knees . . . let me hold it, and weep
    For him, for me, and for all our stricken house.

ORESTES.

    Pylades, give her the urn, and let her weep.
    Whoever she is, she loved Orestes once.
    A friend, perhaps, or one of his own blood?

ELECTRA.

    O ashes of Orestes, dust of the dearest of men!
    Dear ashes, where are all the hopes
    I had when I sent you away? Where are they now?
    You were a torch of hope for all our house,   1130
    And now you are nothing, dust in my hands.
    These hands sent you away, snatched you from death
    And sent you abroad, to strangers. If only
    The gods had prevented me! You would have died
    With our father; you would have shared his death
    And taken your place beside him in the grave.
    But the gods did nothing, and now you have died
    A wretched death abroad, among strangers,
    Far from your sister's care. Whose loving hands
    Washed clean your wounds? Who laid you on the fire,
    Glowing coals weighted with grief?   1140
    They were strangers' hands, not mine:
    Strangers tended you and brought you home,
    Thin ashes in a little urn.

    O Orestes, darling Orestes,
    Do you remembered how I cherished you?
    You were my baby, not hers, not our mother's,
    Not any of the nursemaids' in the palace.
    'Sister,' you called me: I was the only one.
    Now all that is gone, dead on the day you died.   1150
    Like dust on the wind, you have been snatched away.
    Our father is dead; now you have left me too;
    All I had is gone; let me die with you.

Do you hear how our enemies laugh? Do you see
How she dances for joy, the witch-mother
You promised one day to kill? Our black fate,
Orestes, stole that promise forever,
And sent me back, instead of my dear brother,
Dust, ash, a shadow of emptiness.

1160   O my darling,
My dearest darling,
O Orestes,
You are walking a fearful path; and I am dead,
Dead in your death. Take me with you,
Nothing to nothing, inside the grave;
Let me lie with you there forever.
When you were here in the world above, we shared
Everything, you and I. Let me share your death!
Take me with you. There in the world below
1170   Pain ends, and sorrow ends. The dead are at peace.

FIRST WOMAN.
   Electra, my child, remember. Your father
   Was mortal. Orestes was mortal too.
   Do not grieve for them. They paid
   The debt all mortals owe, to death.

ORESTES.
   Now, Pylades, what can I say? What words
   Will help? I can keep silent no longer.

ELECTRA.
   What's the matter? What are you saying, sir?

ORESTES.
   Are you really Electra, princess Electra?

ELECTRA.
   Princess Electra, yes – princess of grief.

ORESTES.
   I am sorry for what has happened –

ELECTRA.
1180   *You* are sorry? Sorry for whom? For me?

ORESTES.
Treated so cruelly, abandoned by the gods –

ELECTRA.
These are words of ill omen, but they are true.

ORESTES.
Kept without a husband, treated like a slave –

ELECTRA.
Sir, we're strangers. Why do you grieve for me?

ORESTES.
For you? For me! I understand at last.

ELECTRA.
My words have made you understand?

ORESTES.
Your words, yes, and the suffering I see.

ELECTRA.
The suffering you see! If that was all – !

ORESTES.
There's worse than this? Is that what you mean?

ELECTRA.
Day and night I must live with murderers.   1190

ORESTES.
What murderers? And who was murdered? Speak.

ELECTRA.
They murdered my father, and made me a slave.

ORESTES.
You must name them, Electra: name the criminals.

ELECTRA.
Her name is: mother. The name is all she has.

ORESTES.
How does she ill-treat you? Does she beat you? Starve
                                                        you?

ELECTRA.
She is wicked and cruel in everything she does.

ORESTES.
Will no one help you, no one take your part?

ELECTRA.
There was one, once. You brought his ashes home.

ORESTES.
Unhappy Electra! I pity you –

ELECTRA.
1200   If you pity me, you are alone on earth.

ORESTES.
Yes – alone on earth, I share your suffering.

ELECTRA.
You share it? How? Are you a distant kinsman – ?

ORESTES.
I would say more . . . These women: can I trust them?

ELECTRA.
They're good friends. You can trust them. Speak.

ORESTES.
If you give me back the urn, I will explain.

ELECTRA.
No! No! I beg you, don't ask me that.

ORESTES.
Do as I ask. No harm will come of it.

ELECTRA.
My brother's ashes . . . they're all I have . . .

ORESTES.
Give me the urn.

ELECTRA.
O Orestes, darling Orestes,
1210   You are stolen away, cheated of burial . . .

ORESTES.
Enough. There's no need to talk of burial.

ELECTRA.
No need . . . ? When my brother is dead?

ORESTES.
That's not the way to think of him now.

ELECTRA.
Does my dear dead brother reject me too?

ORESTES.
No one rejects you. There is no need to mourn.

ELECTRA.
But his ashes . . . I held them in my hands.

ORESTES.
Those were not his ashes. It was a lie.

ELECTRA.
Where is he buried, then? Where is his grave?

ORESTES.
He has no grave. The living have no graves.

ELECTRA.
The living? Oh . . . ! You say –

ORESTES.
It's the truth.   1220

ELECTRA.
Orestes is alive?

ORESTES.
As *I* live, *he* lives.

ELECTRA.
You are Orestes?

ORESTES.
Look, Electra:
Our father's ring . . . Agamemnon's ring. Look.

ELECTRA.
O my dear . . . my darling . . .

ORESTES.
Electra . . . sister . . .

ELECTRA.
Your dear voice . . . you have come home . . .

ORESTES.
I have come home.

ELECTRA.
Let me hold you . . . kiss you . . . forever . . .

ORESTES.
Forever.

ELECTRA.
O my dear friends, women of Argos, look:
Orestes died, they said, and it was a trick –
Now another trick, and he's alive again.

FIRST WOMAN.
1230   We see him, child; and for this happiness
Tears of relief and joy run down our cheeks.

ELECTRA.
O my brother,
My dear father's son,
Suddenly, beyond all hope,
You have come, you are home.

ORESTES.
Electra, hush –

ELECTRA.
What is it?

ORESTES.
They'll hear inside.

ELECTRA.
By Artemis
Queen of heaven,
1240   I'll never fear them

Again, those women,
Those parasites, inside.

ORESTES.
Remember: Ares the war-god lives
In women too – as you have seen.

ELECTRA.
Don't speak of it!
The grief, the misery
That tortures me
Endlessly, beyond all cure.   1250

ORESTES.
The time will come.
We'll remember, and punish them.

ELECTRA.
I must speak!
In Justice's name
I must tell my suffering.
We're safe now: let me speak.

ORESTES.
Electra, soon –

ELECTRA.
When? When?

ORESTES.
Soon will be time: not now.

ELECTRA.
Now you're home –   1260
Beyond hope or thought
You're home. Who
Would keep silent now?
Who would not shout for joy?

ORESTES.
The gods spoke. The time has come.
The murderers must pay the price.

ELECTRA.
Sing, then, for joy!

If the gods have spoken,
If the gods have brought you home
1270   To Argos, sing for joy!

ORESTES.
Electra, hush! When the murderers
Are punished, it will be time to sing.

ELECTRA.
I waited, I watched
Your dear road home.
At last you came:
The long misery is done.
O Orestes, never leave me,
Never leave me again.

ORESTES.
No one will part us now.

ELECTRA.
1280   Do you swear it?

ORESTES.
Forever.

ELECTRA.
O my friends, when I heard
My brother's voice, the dear voice
I thought never to hear again,
How could I not sing for joy?
He has come home, my dear one,
My darling, the brother I longed for.

ORESTES.
Say no more now. Tell me later
The story of all our mother's crimes,
1290   How Aegisthus squanders the royal wealth
And sucks the storehouse dry. Tell me later:
There's too much to hear, and time is short.

Tell me this, now: just this I need to know.
How can we best attack them? Openly,
Or secretly, lying in wait, to put
An end to their smiling for evermore?

When Pylades and I have gone inside,
Your job will be to trick our mother. Hide
Your smiles of happiness, or she will know.
You must weep tears, tears for the dreadful news.
When we have succeeded, then you can smile.   1300

ELECTRA.
Dearest brother, you know I'm in your hands.
What you want, I want. You're all
My happiness; without you there is none.
I would not hurt you, not for all the world.
The gods are helping us. Our time is now.

You must know how things are in Argos:
Aegisthus is away, and our mother rules.
Our mother! I'll trick her, never fear.
No smiles, no happiness: I'll remember   1310
The hate that has eaten my life away,
And I'll show her tears. Look, Orestes,
They are tears of joy. In a single day
You have come home to Argos twice, first dead
And now alive. For me, it is like
A miracle. If Father came back
And stood beside me now, I'd say
He was really there, he was not a ghost.
That's how you, now, appear to me. Tell me
What I must do to help. When you were dead,
And I was alone, I would have made my choice   1320
A glorious victory or a glorious death.

ORESTES.
Be quiet now. Someone's coming. I can hear them
There at the palace door.

ELECTRA.
Go inside.
You bring them misery, not joy –
And it is a gift they cannot refuse.

  Enter ORESTES' SERVANT.

SERVANT.
Orestes, Electra! You're like little children!

Are you tired of living? Have you lost
What common sense you had? You're in danger,
Deadly danger – not soon, but here and now.
1330   Can't you see it? If I had not been here,
Keeping watch at the door, your words, your
        plans,
Would have been inside the palace before you.
You have me to thank for preventing it.
Have done with your speeches, your endless cries
Of joy. There's work to be done. Delay now
Will be fatal. Go inside, and finish it.

ORESTES.
And when I'm inside, what will I find?

SERVANT.
1340   It's safe. No one will recognise you.

ORESTES.
You've convinced them, then, that I am dead?

SERVANT.
They all believe it: you are dead and gone.

ORESTES.
What did they say? Were they glad to hear it?

SERVANT.
When it's done, I'll tell you. As things are now,
They think they're safe, and they ask no more.

ELECTRA.
Orestes, please tell me, who is this man?

ORESTES.
Don't you recognise him?

ELECTRA.
Not clearly, no.

ORESTES.
He's the man you chose to save my life.

ELECTRA.
To save . . . ? You mean – ?

ORESTES.
　Long ago, you made him
　Take me to Phocis, to a safe hiding-place.　　　　　1350

ELECTRA.
　This is the same man? The only man in Argos
　Loyal to our father on the day he died?

ORESTES.
　The same man: no need of proof.

ELECTRA.
　O dearest of men! Our saviour, the saviour
　Of Agamemnon's house, have you come home at
　　　last?
　Is it really you? You have saved our lives;
　You have ended our misery forever.
　God bless the hands and feet that helped us so!
　You were here, beside me in the palace,
　And you gave me no sign: you broke my heart
　With false stories, when all the time　　　　　　1360
　You were bringing the news I longed to hear.
　O let me embrace you, let me call you father –
　My dear friend, on this one day
　Most hated and dearest of men to me.

SERVANT.
　No more now. For all that has happened,
　Electra, there will be many nights and days
　To tell the story. Now, we must act.
　Orestes and Pylades, the time is now:
　The queen is alone, no soldiers are near.
　Delay now, and you'll have to face　　　　　　1370
　An army of guards, well-trained and well-armed.

ORESTES.
　Come inside, Pylades. The talking, the planning,
　Is done. It's time. The gods are watching,
　The guardians of Argos, here at the gate.
　We honour them, and ask them to help us now.

　　ORESTES and PYLADES exeunt.

ELECTRA.
    Lord Apollo, hear them; grant their prayers.
    I'm your servant; I've given you
    What gifts I had. Apollo, hear me now.
    On my knees I beg you,
1380   Beseech you to help us.
    Smile on us. Make our plans come true.
    The gods have set a price on human wickedness:
    Show all men, now, how it is paid!

WOMEN.
    Ares the hunter, the war-god, is here.
    He pants for blood. There is no escape.
    Furies pad through the palace halls.
    They have the scent. There is no escape.
    The vision of hope
    That fluttered in my heart
1390   Lives: it will soon come true.

    Orestes, champion of the dead, is here,
    Stealthy inside the palace halls,
    His father's rich palace of old.
    Hermes, shepherd of souls,
    Whispered secret ways.
    It is not soon: it is now!

ELECTRA.
    Hush, women; hush, friends. Listen:
    The men are at work. It is now.

FIRST WOMAN.
1400   What's happening? Tell us . . . tell us.

ELECTRA.
    She is preparing the urn for burial.
    They are beside her. It is now.

FIRST WOMAN.
    Why are you not inside, to help?

ELECTRA.
    I must stand on guard;
    I must watch for Aegisthus.

CLYTEMNESTRA (*inside*).
Ah! Assassins! Help me!
Is there no one to help me?

ELECTRA.
Inside. She's screaming. Can you hear?

FIRST WOMAN.
We hear the death-cry;
We hear, and shudder.

CLYTEMNESTRA.
Oh . . . Oh! Aegisthus, help me!

ELECTRA.
Another cry.

CLYTEMNESTRA.
My son, O my son! Have pity . . .   1410

ELECTRA.
Yes! As you pitied him!
As you pitied his father!

FIRST WOMAN.
People of Argos, children of Atreus,
The ancient curse is lifted, lifted.

CLYTEMNESTRA.
Ah!

ELECTRA.
Three blows. The laws demand three blows.

CLYTEMNESTRA.
Ah!

ELECTRA.
We must wait for Aegisthus now.

WOMEN.
The curse is a living thing:
Dead men rise from the grave,
Dead men of old, to drink   1420
The blood of those who murdered them.

FIRST WOMAN.
Look: they are here. Crimson hands . . .
A sacrifice. The debt is paid.

Re-enter ORESTES *and* PYLADES.

ELECTRA.
Orestes . . .

ORESTES.
It is all right. Inside, it is all right,
If Apollo's prophecy is kept.

ELECTRA.
The . . . woman . . . is dead?

ORESTES.
Our mother is dead. Her pride,
Her cruelty . . . forget your fear.

FIRST WOMAN.
1430   My children, look: Aegisthus
Is coming. He is here.

ELECTRA.
Orestes, Pylades, hurry . . .

ORESTES.
Where is he? Can you see him?

FIRST WOMAN.
Yes; he's coming up from the town.
He's smiling . . . he suspects nothing.

ELECTRA.
Go back inside; wait for him there.
The gods helped you before – pray
That they are near to help you now.

ORESTES.
Never fear: we're ready.

ELECTRA.
Leave all the rest to me.

ORESTES *and* PYLADES *return inside.*

FIRST WOMAN.
Honey his ears with words
To welcome a royal king;
Let him suspect nothing   1440
Till Justice's trap is sprung.

Enter AEGISTHUS.

AEGISTHUS.
Where are the strangers from Phocis?
The ones who brought news of Orestes' death
In a shipwreck of chariots. Answer me.
You! Yes, you. Electra. Where are they?
What? Silent? You had so much to say before.
Tell me. He was your brother: you must know.

ELECTRA.
Of course I know. My own brother – the brother
I loved more than all the world! Of course I know.

AEGISTHUS.
Answer me, then. Where are the strangers from   1450
Phocis?

ELECTRA.
Inside, with the queen. They went straight to her heart.

AEGISTHUS.
And is it true, their story, that he is dead?

ELECTRA.
It's truer than words: they brought him back.

AEGISTHUS.
I must see the body, see it for myself.

ELECTRA.
See it, if you must. It's there to see.

AEGISTHUS.
At last you've said something that pleases me.

ELECTRA.
Be pleased then, if it pleases you so much.

AEGISTHUS.
Be quiet. Slaves, open the doors, and show
All the people what there is to see, inside.

The doors of the palace are opened. CLYTEMNESTRA's
body, covered with a cloth, is revealed. ORESTES *and*
PYLADES *stand beside it.*

1460   People of Argos, look! The empty hopes
He gave you once are dead. Learn from this corpse
To bow to my yoke, to accept the bit.
Disobey, and you will suffer. Learn that now!

ELECTRA.
My lesson is learned. I have understood,
At last, to accept what I cannot change.

AEGISTHUS.
O Zeus, the hand of god was here: justice,
More than we can understand, is done.
Uncover the face. I am a relative,
And I must pay the dead my last respects.

ORESTES.
1470   Lift the cloth yourself. It is your duty,
Not mine, to view the corpse and say farewell.

AEGISTHUS.
You're right. Slave, go inside: ask the queen to come.

ORESTES.
There is no need to fetch her. She is here.

    AEGISTHUS *lifts the cloth.*

AEGISTHUS.
O gods! What sight is this?

ORESTES.
Look, and see. Are you afraid?

AEGISTHUS.
Who are you? Answer? What trap is this?

ORESTES.
You called me dead; I am alive again.

AEGISTHUS.
Orestes! God help me. Now I understand.   1480

ORESTES.
Priest-king! Prophet-king! At last you see!

AEGISTHUS.
My death is near: there is no escape.
Before you kill me, let me say this –

ELECTRA.
No, Orestes, no! Let him say nothing!
He's in the noose, the trap is sprung –
What good will it do
To allow him a little time? Kill him now,
At once – and throw his corpse
For dogs to maul, out of our sight.
He has brought us pain and misery:
Punish him! Kill him now, as he deserves!   1490

ORESTES.
Go inside, you, quickly. The answer now
Is not more words: it is your death.

AEGISTHUS.
Why must we go inside? If what you're doing
Is right, why hide it? Murder me out here!

ORESTES.
Give no more orders. Go inside.
Where you killed my father, there you must die.

AEGISTHUS.
The palace of the children of Atreus!
Must it see death after death, for evermore?

ORESTES.
It will see yours. That much, at least, is sure.

AEGISTHUS.
And what of your own death, if you kill me?   1500
I die for your father – you will die for me.

ORESTES.
Still you invent arguments! Go inside.
It is time.

AEGISTHUS.
Lead the way.

ORESTES.
No: you must go first.

AEGISTHUS.
In case I escape?

ORESTES.
No. You must not know,
Or choose, the exact moment of your death.
You must suffer, and suffer to the end.
A sharp, sudden death: if that was the price
All criminals paid, there would soon be no more crime.

Exeunt AEGISTHUS *and* ORESTES.

WOMEN.
Children of Atreus, from great suffering
You have won freedom at last
1510   By what has been done here, today.

PHILOCTETES

Translated by Kenneth McLeish

Characters

ODYSSEUS
NEOPTOLEMOS
PHILOCTETES
TRADER, a disguised servant of Odysseus
HERACLES
CHORUS OF SAILORS FROM NEOPTOLEMOS' SHIP

This translation of *Philoctetes* was performed by Cheek by Jowl at the Donmar Warehouse, London, and on nationwide and world tours in 1989. The cast was as follows:

ODYSSEUS	Charlie Roe
NEOPTOLEMOS	Paterson Joseph
PHILOCTETES	Keith Bartlett
MERCHANT	Trevor Baxter
HERACLES	Duncan Duff
CHORUS	Peter Darling
	Duncan Duff, Michael Jenn, Lloyd Owen,
	Cecilia Noble, Dale Rapley, Timothy Walker

Directed by Declan Donellan

A seashore. In the background, a cave.

Enter ODYSSEUS *and* NEOPTOLEMOS, *with a*
SERVANT

ODYSSEUS.
   This is the coast of Lemnos, a barren island
   In the midst of empty sea. No one lives here.
   Look, Neoptolemos, son of Achilles, son
   Of the noblest of the Greeks; this is the place
   I chose to maroon him, years ago –
   Philoctetes of Malis, son of Poias.

   I was obeying orders from our generals.
   His foot was festering, oozing pus
   From a foul wound. Even at festivals
   We hardly dared touch the wine or meat:
   He gave us no peace; day and night, he filled   10
   The whole camp with groans and curses, cries
   Of ill omen that spoiled the sacrifice.

   But no more of that now. If he hears us,
   If he finds out we are here, the plan
   I have made to capture him will fail.
   Your part is to help me. Look around
   Till you find a cave with two entrances –
   Two suntraps to sit in when it is cold,
   And a passage between them, to sleep in
   In summer, cooled by the breeze. Below it,
   On the left, you should find a spring   20
   Of fresh water, if it has not dried up.
   Go quietly. Signal if he is there.
   Then I'll tell you what we must do next.

NEOPTOLEMOS.
   Odysseus, sir! This *is* the right place.
   I think I see the cave you mean.

ODYSSEUS.
   Where is it? Above you, or further down?

NEOPTOLEMOS.
   Up here. Deserted, silent. No one is here.

ODYSSEUS.

30   Look inside. He may be inside, asleep.

NEOPTOLEMOS.
It's empty. There's no one about.

ODYSSEUS.
Does anyone live there? Are there signs of that?

NEOPTOLEMOS.
Yes: a bed of leaves, where someone sleeps.

ODYSSEUS.
Is there anything else? Go further in.

NEOPTOLEMOS.
A cup, roughly carved from a block of wood –
Not by a craftsman. And twigs, for a fire.

ODYSSEUS.
This must be the cave. He must live here.

NEOPTOLEMOS.
Look! Bandages. The rags he wears to bind his wound.
Rolled carefully – but foul with pus.

ODYSSEUS.

40   This is the cave. He can't be far away.
A sick man, crippled by that old wound –
He couldn't get far. He's gone foraging,
For food, or some soothing herb he knows.
Leave your servant up there to stand on guard,
In case Philoctetes takes us by surprise.
He'd like to catch me, more than any Greek alive.

    Exit SERVANT.

NEOPTOLEMOS.
He's gone further up. He'll guard the path.
Now, lord Odysseus, what must we do next?

ODYSSEUS.

50   Son of Achilles, I'm asking you
For courage first, and then obedience.
Whatever I tell you, however strange,

You must do it at once. That's why you came.

NEOPTOLEMOS.
What must I do?

ODYSSEUS.
You must cheat Philoctetes,
And tangle his soul in a net of words.
He'll ask who you are, where you are from.
Begin with the truth: you are Neoptolemos,
Son of Achilles. Then say you are sailing home,
Away from the Greeks, in a furious rage:
They begged you, persuaded you to go to Troy;   60
Only then, they said, could they hope to win.
But when you asked them for your father's arms –
The armour of Achilles, yours by right –
They refused, and gave it to Odysseus.

Tell him that. Call me any names you like.
Spare me no insults. He must believe you,
Or else you bring ruin on all the Greeks.
For we must have his bow;
Without it, you'll never capture Troy.

Are you surprised that he'll believe *you*,
Trust *you*, rather than me? This is the reason.   70
You took no part in the first expedition;
You are your own free man; you are not bound
By oaths of loyalty; you sailed with us
Of your own free will. For me, none of that
Is true. If he sees me, and has the bow,
He'll kill us both. The bow gives him power
That no one else can match. Force is useless.
That's why you must trick him, and steal the bow.

My dear boy, I know how unused you are
To this talk of stealing and trickery.   80
But the prize is worth it – the fall of Troy!
Take the risk. The future will prove us right.
For one little day, for one dishonest hour,
Do as I say. When it is done, your life
Can be the noblest the world has ever seen.

NEOPTOLEMOS.
  My lord Odysseus, even to talk of it
  Is painful. How can I ever do it?
  I am Achilles' son, noblest of Greeks –
  How can I cheat and steal to get my way?
90 I'll conquer by force, not trickery.
  The man is outnumbered, a poor cripple -
  If he fights, he'll lose. I know
  I was sent to help you, to obey you;
  But with respect, my lord, I'd rather
  Fight fair and lose than cheat and win.

ODYSSEUS.
  So like your father! When I was a young man
  I was just like you: action, not argument.
  But now I have learned from experience
  That blows sometimes miss; words always win.

NEOPTOLEMOS.
100 Have you more orders – or is lying enough?

ODYSSEUS.
  Your orders are these – play a trick, and win.

NEOPTOLEMOS.
  And if I persuade him without a trick?

ODYSSEUS.
  You won't. Persuasion, just like force, will fail.

NEOPTOLEMOS.
  Is he so dangerous? Has he such power?

ODYSSEUS.
  He has arrows of death that never miss.

NEOPTOLEMOS.
  To speak to him at all is dangerous.

ODYSSEUS.
  Not if you trick him. There is no other way.

NEOPTOLEMOS.
  But . . . to lie! How can you approve of that?

ODYSSEUS.
  If we lie, we're safe. I approve of that.

NEOPTOLEMOS.
  I must look him in the face, and lie to him?   110

ODYSSEUS.
  It's for your own good. Remember that.

NEOPTOLEMOS.
  What good will it do me, if he comes to Troy?

ODYSSEUS.
  With his bow, and his arrows, Troy will fall.

NEOPTOLEMOS.
  The oracle said that I would capture Troy.

ODYSSEUS.
  Using his weapons, yes. Without them, no.

NEOPTOLEMOS.
  We must take him, then. There is no other choice.

ODYSSEUS.
  Do it, and you'll win a double prize.

NEOPTOLEMOS.
  What prize? Tell me. I might not still refuse.

ODYSSEUS.
  To be called noble and wise: that is the prize.

NEOPTOLEMOS.
  Very well. I refuse no longer. I agree.   120

ODYSSEUS.
  You understand clearly what you have to do?

NEOPTOLEMOS.
  It's clear enough. I understand.

ODYSSEUS.
  Stay here, then, and wait for him. I'll go:
  He must not see me with you. Your servant
  Up there must come back to the ship with me.
  If things go slowly here, I'll send him back

Disguised as a ship's captain, to help the trick.
130   We'll find some clever tale for him to tell –
And whatever he says, go along with it,
Make use of it. I'll go now, back to the ship.
The rest is up to you. And may Hermes
God of trickery guide us, with Athena,
Goddess of victory, who watches over me.

Exit ODYSSEUS *enter the* CHORUS *of* SAILORS.

A SAILOR.
    Sir, we are strangers, in a strange land.
    If we meet that sharp, suspicious man,
    Tell us what to hide, and what to say.

ANOTHER.
    Princes, who rule in Zeus' name,
    Are gifted more than other mortals:
140   They're subtle, they decide, they know.

ANOTHER.
    Sir, you are a prince, with royal power
    Inherited from kings of long ago.
    Tell us your orders. We will obey.

NEOPTOLEMOS.
    Look around now: he's not here.
    This is his lair, on the island's edge.
    Look your fill. But when he comes back,
    The outlaw, the castaway,
    Keep hidden and watch, in case
    I signal suddenly for help.

FIRST SAILOR.
150   Sir, we'll protect you, keep an eye
    On you, as we have always done.
    Your safety's our first concern.

SECOND SAILOR.
    Tell us this first: where does he live?
    Where should we look? We must take care:
    He may be hiding, waiting to attack.

THIRD SAILOR.
  Show us his haunts, his tracks,
  His lair. Does he sleep rough,
  Or under cover? Tell us where to look.

NEOPTOLEMOS.
  Look, up there: a nest in the rock,
  Two entrances –   160

FIRST SAILOR.
  Poor wretch. Is he inside?

NEOPTOLEMOS.
  He'll be out hunting,
  Shuffling in pain along these paths,
  Shooting deadly arrows:
  Soul-sick, they say, with pain,
  With gnawing agony
  No one will cure.

SAILORS.
  We pity him.
  He is alone, and full of pain.   170
  There is no one
  To talk to him or care for him.
  He is eaten with pain,
  Baffled by each new day.
  How can he bear it?
  He is mortal: his fate
  Was chosen by the gods.
  Weep for the miseries of mortals.
  Whose burden is endless pain.

  Was he rich?   180
  A nobleman's son, perhaps,
  Second to none?
  Now he's nothing: alone
  With the beasts of woods and hills.
  He is starving,
  Twisted with pain,
  How can he bear it?
  No one hears his bitterness:

Only Echo, chuckling in the hills,
190   Answers his cries.

NEOPTOLEMOS.
His sufferings are nothing strange.
I know they were sent by the gods.
He was marooned here alone
To soothe the savage rage
Of Chryse, and fulfil the plans
The gods made for Troy. His arrows
Are deadly: no one can escape.
When the time comes, Troy will fall
By them – and it is Heaven's will
200   That until then, he must stay here.

FIRST SAILOR.
Listen!

NEOPTOLEMOS.
What is it?

FIRST SAILOR.
I heard a groan,
The cry of a man in pain.
From this side. No, this.
There it is again. A man
Dragging himself along,
Moaning with pain. A sick man,
A cripple. It's plain enough.
My lord –

NEOPTOLEMOS.
210   What is it?

FIRST SAILOR.
Think what to do:
He's nearly here. Listen:
This is no shepherd
Whistling as he goes along –
It's a man in torment,
Groaning, stumbling
His way on an empty shore.

Enter PHILOCTETES. *He carries a bow.*

PHILOCTETES.
Strangers!
Who are you? Where have you come from? Why   220
Have you put in here, to this empty place?
There is nothing here: no shelter, no people.
What country are you from? What people?
From your clothes, you look like Greeks,
The most welcome sight in all the world.

If only you'd speak. Don't be afraid.
I look like a savage beast, more than a man.
Pity me. An outlaw, a castaway.
Alone, in pain. If you mean me no harm,
If you're my friends, speak to me. Answer,   230
Please answer. I ask for nothing else.

NEOPTOLEMOS.
Of course I'll answer. And first of all,
The words you most hoped to hear: we are Greeks.

PHILOCTETES.
No words are more welcome in all the world.
Greeks! After all these years . . . and you are Greeks!
My boy . . . my dear boy . . . why have you come here?
Is there something here you want? Something you need?
Or were you blown off course, in a lucky storm?
O my boy, answer me. Tell me who you are.

NEOPTOLEMOS.
I come from the island of Scyros.
I am sailing home. My name is Neoptolemos,   240
Son of Achilles. There: you know it all.

PHILOCTETES.
Achilles' son? I was his dearest friend.
I loved Scyros. I knew your guardian, too,
When your father left for Troy. But why
Have you come here? Where did your journey start?

NEOPTOLEMOS.
In Troy. I am sailing home from Troy.

PHILOCTETES.
> How can that be? You were not with us then,
> Years ago, when our army left for Troy.

NEOPTOLEMOS.
> When our army left . . . ? You mean *you* were at Troy?

PHILOCTETES.
> Don't you know me? Don't you recognise me?

NEOPTOLEMOS.
250 > How could I recognise a man I've never met?

PHILOCTETES.
> Have you never heard my name? Never heard
> Of the wrongs I suffer, the pain I bear?

NEOPTOLEMOS.
> No. Every word you say is new to me.

PHILOCTETES.
> O gods! Is there more? More misery to bear?
> Ten years twisted with pain – and no one knows
> How I suffer, no one in the whole of Greece!
> My wound feeds and grows stronger every day –
> Is it still a secret, a private joke
> To the criminals, cursed by the gods, who left me here?

260 > Neoptolemos, son of Achilles:
> I think you have heard of me. I am the man
> Who was made master of the bow of Heracles –
> Philoctetes, son of Poias. I am the man
> Our generals and Odysseus of Ithaca
> Banished to this empty place, the man gnawed
> By a vicious sickness, marked out for death
> By the murderous fangs of a deadly snake.

> They left me to endure it: here, alone.
> They sailed away and left me. We had come
270 > From the island of Chryse – a hard voyage
> In stormy seas. I was exhausted,
> And fell asleep in a cave here on the headland.
> At once, overjoyed, they seized their chance
> And sailed. Oh, they left me a supply of rags,

Beggar's rags, and a little store of food.
God curse them! God send them the same one day!

Can you imagine what it was like to wake up
And find them gone? Can you imagine my tears,
My despair? The warfleet I took to Troy,
Stolen away; its captain marooned, alone,   280
A helpless cripple racked with pain. I looked
For a living soul to help. I searched the island.
There was no one. Nothing. All I had was pain.

So the years passed: season after season.
No one came. I am the master; I am the slave.
I just keep alive. When my belly needs food,
The bow provides it: birds, shot on the wing.
The arrows never miss, but whatever I shoot   290
I have to fetch myself, crawling, dragging
This foot. Sometimes in winter the pools freeze:
If I want water to drink, I must light
A fire. Then I must crawl to fetch wood,
And if the old embers are dead, strike flint
On stone to unlock the secret spark.
Shelter, and fire. I keep alive. What more
Do I need, but an end to my endless pain?

My boy, do you know what this island is like?   300
No sailors land here by choice. Why should they?
There are no harbours, no markets, no towns.
A sensible traveller keeps well away.

But now and then, as the years pass, crews put in here
By accident. When they do, they pity me –
Or so they say. They leave me charity:
A little food, say, or some cast-off clothes.
But that other thing, when I mention it –
To be taken home – they never give me that.   310

A living death. I have been here ten years.
I pine, I starve, only my sickness thrives.
This is the handiwork of the sons of Atreus
And of proud Odysseus. May the gods above
Punish them one day with suffering like mine.

FIRST SAILOR.
> Like everyone else who comes here
> I pity you, Philoctetes, I pity you.

NEOPTOLEMOS.
> The sons of Atreus! Proud Odysseus!
320   Every word you say is true. I know
> Their arrogance. Their evil has touched me too.

PHILOCTETES.
> They are evil men, cursed by the gods.
> How have they harmed you? What debt do they
>   owe?

NEOPTOLEMOS.
> A debt of suffering they will pay in full.
> Mycenae and Sparta will learn, one day,
> That Scyros, too, breeds fighting men.

PHILOCTETES.
> Well said, boy! Good. But why do you hate them?
> Tell me. What lodged such fury in your heart?

NEOPTOLEMOS.
> I'll tell you, hard though it is: how I came
330   To Troy, and how they mocked and insulted me.
> When Fate decreed Achilles had to die –

PHILOCTETES.
> What? Achilles, dead? Tell me clearly:
> Achilles son of Peleus, your father, is dead?

NEOPTOLEMOS.
> Yes, he is dead – and by no mortal hand.
> They say Apollo killed him, the archer god.

PHILOCTETES.
> His will be done. And now, Neoptolemos
> Son of Achilles, what should I do? Listen
> To your story, or weep for your father's death?

NEOPTOLEMOS.
> Already you have cause enough to weep
340   For your own sake. You need not weep for him.

PHILOCTETES.
What you say is true. I accept it. Tell me, then:
How did those noble lords insult you?

NEOPTOLEMOS.
They came to fetch me from Scyros, in a ship
Fluttering with flags: noble Odysseus
And Phoinix, my father's old guardian.
They said – and it could have been true or false –
That with my father dead, the gods had decreed
That I, and only I, was to capture Troy.

That was their story. They soon persuaded me
To sail with them. There were two reasons. First,
My father, the father I had never seen.   350
His body was laid out for burial:
I wanted to touch him and weep for him.
And second, I was flattered. To think
That I, and I alone, was to capture Troy!

So we set sail. Wind and the sailors' oars
Brought us in two days to cruel Sigeum.
I went ashore. The soldiers crowded round
To welcome me. 'He's Achilles!' they said,
'He's Achilles come to life again!'
But Achilles my father was dead, laid out
For burial. I mourned him as custom demands.   360
Then I went to the sons of Atreus, my friends
(Or so I thought), and asked for my father's arms
And whatever else was his. For answer
They laughed at me, laughed in my face, and said,
'The arms of Achilles! Everything else
Is yours to take. But his arms have been given
To another man: to Odysseus, Laertes' son.'
Tears of fury burned my eyes. I leapt up,
Blazing, and shouted at them. 'How dare you?
How dare you give my arms to another man
Without my leave? How dare you insult me so?'   370
At that Odysseus said – he was standing by –
'Now now, my boy. The arms are mine by right.
I earned them when I saved your father's life.'

I was furious. I cursed him. I called down
Every insult I knew. That he should steal my arms!
He's a mild man, but at last I stung him
Into answering. 'Your place was here with us,
Fighting the Trojans – and you stayed away.
380   Insult me how you like, boast how you like,
You'll never sail home and take those arms.'

So, insulted and mocked, empty-handed,
I am sailing home. Odysseus took from me
What was rightly mine. The lord Odysseus!
Lord of deceit. And what of them, the generals,
The commanders, the sons of Atreus?
As a city looks to its king, so men
In battle look to their generals to lead them well.
If the slave's corrupt, the master is to blame.

That's my story. Whoever hates
The sons of Atreus is my friend,
390   And the gods' friend, for evermore.

SAILORS.
Mother Earth,
Mother of Zeus himself;
Queen of the wide river,
Pactolus of golden sands;
You ride in majesty,
Your chariot drawn
400   By a team of hunting lions.

Earth-mother, Queen,
I called you to witness then,
When the sons of Atreus in their pride
Over-ruled this man,
When they gave his father's arms,
A wonder of the world,
To Odysseus, Laertes' son.

PHILOCTETES.
Neoptolemos, you bring a convincing tale
Of lies and insults. Everything you say
Fits what I knew of them, the sons of Atreus

And Odysseus lord of deceit, who bends
His tongue to any lie, any trick
Right or wrong, that will bring him what he wants.
I know them: I'm not surprised. But where   410
Was Ajax? He is an honest man: he
Could have stopped them. Why didn't he speak up?

NEOPTOLEMOS.
Ajax is dead. If he'd been still alive
I'd not have been robbed; I'd have the arms.

PHILOCTETES.
Ajax, dead? Have the gods taken him as well?

NEOPTOLEMOS.
Yes he's dead. He lies in the underworld.

PHILOCTETES.
Why should he die, and not those criminals?
Diomedes son of Tydeus, Odysseus –
Why don't they die? They should never have lived.

NEOPTOLEMOS.
They live and thrive. They are princes of men,
The glory of all the fighting-men of Greece.   420

PHILOCTETES.
And Nestor, King of Pylos – what news of him?
He was an old friend, a good, honest man.
His wise advice often stopped their wickedness.

NEOPTOLEMOS.
He too has suffered. He has lost his son,
Antilochus, who sailed with him to Troy.

PHILOCTETES.
Antilochus too! You have told me of the deaths
Of two good friends. What is left for us now,
What can we hope for, if Antilochus
And Ajax, who should have lived, are dead,
And Odysseus, who should be dead, still lives?   430

NEOPTOLEMOS.
He's a skilful wrestler, who has survived

Till now. But even skilful wrestlers fall.

PHILOCTETES.
In god's name, Neoptolemos! Was Patroclus
Not there to help you? Your father's dearest friend.

NEOPTOLEMOS.
He too is dead. And it is always so,
Philoctetes – the wicked never die
In war, except by chance. Only good men die.

PHILOCTETES.
In that case, give me news of one wicked man:
That vile creature with the clever tongue,
440   So expert in arguing. Is he alive?

NEOPTOLEMOS.
I don't understand. Do you mean Odysseus?

PHILOCTETES.
Not Odysseus, no. There was another one.
His name was Thersites. No one could stop him
Talking and arguing. Is he still alive?

NEOPTOLEMOS.
I don't know him. I've not heard he is dead.

PHILOCTETES.
Nothing evil has died, in this whole war.
The gods in their wisdom look after them;
450   It pleases them; they close the gates of Hades
To cheats and criminals, as if there was room
In the underworld only for honest men.
How can we understand? How can we praise
The gods, if we cannot praise the things they do?

NEOPTOLEMOS.
Philoctetes, my part in this is done.
From now on I'll watch the Trojan War
And the sons of Atreus from far away.
Now that honest men are dead and liars thrive,
Now that heroes are beaten and cowards rule,
I'll not stay to see it: I'll go back

To stony Scyros, and live content at home.   460
Now I must go to the ship. Philoctetes,
I leave you with the blessing of the gods.
May they answer your prayers, and cure your sickness.
Men, we must go. When the gods send fair wind,
We must be ready to set sail at once.

PHILOCTETES.
Neoptolemos! Will you go so soon?

NEOPTOLEMOS.
Yes. The wind's freshening. It's time.
We must go on board, and make ready at once.

PHILOCTETES.
Neoptolemos, I beg you, in the name
Of your father and mother, and all you hold dear
At home, I beg you, don't leave me here   470
Alone. You've seen how I suffer. You've heard
All the miseries I endure. Pity me.
Find a corner of your heart and pity me.

I know I'm not the cargo you would choose
To have on board – but bear me, put up with me!
You're a good man. Be kind, not cruel. Think
How your honour will suffer if you leave me here,
The glory and fame if you take me home.

I'll not trouble you long: less than one day.   480
Take me to the ship, and stow me where you like –
The stern, the hold, the prow, out of the way,
Wherever I will least offend the crew.

Say yes. I beg you in god's name, say yes.
Do as I ask. Look: I'm on my knees,
A sick man, a cripple. Don't leave me here,
Marooned alone in this desert. Pity me,
Take me to Scyros, home with you, or else
To the mainland, to Euboea, from where
It is just a little step home for me   490
To the hills of Trachis, the plain of Spercheius.
Home! To my dear father, if he's still alive.
I have sent him so many messages

By passing travellers: prayers to come himself
Or send a ship and crew to rescue me.
But no one came. He's dead, perhaps, or else
(And I think it more likely) my messengers
Cared nothing for me, and made their own way home.

500   Now you have come: messenger, rescuer, all
In one. I beg you, save me, pity me.
Remember, chance governs all human life.
When it's good, when we're up, we must look out
For trouble ahead, or we may come crashing down.

SAILORS.
Pity him, sir. He has told
Of unbearable suffering.
Pray god none of those we love
Ever has to suffer so.
If you hate them, sir,
510   The cruel sons of Atreus,
Turn the evil they have done
To this man to good.
Take him on board;
Take him swiftly home
Where he so longs to be.
Pity him, sir –
Help him, and be spared
The anger of the gods.

NEOPTOLEMOS.
It's easy now to stand by and pity him.
520   But once he's on board, when you're sick of the stench
Of his wound, will you be so generous then?

FIRST SAILOR.
Yes, sir. We understand, we accept him.
We'll not change. No one will blame us for that.

NEOPTOLEMOS.
When my men are so kind, so generous,
How can I refuse? If you agree, we sail.
Philoctetes, we'll take you on board.
Go to the ship, as quickly as you can.

O gods, grant us a safe journey – safe
Passage from here, a safe voyage home.

PHILOCTETES.

O blessed light of day. O dear boy . . .   530
Dear friends . . . how can I prove my gratitude?
Let us go, at once. Let us kiss goodbye
To this place, this dreadful place. I called it home.
Home! How did I bear it? Look for yourself –
The sight alone would frighten other men,
But I had to endure it; I had no choice;
Long suffering taught me patience in the end.

FIRST SAILOR.

Look, my lords: two men, coming from the ship.
One of the crew, sir, and another man,   540
A stranger. What is it? We must wait, and hear.

Enter a SAILOR *and the* SERVANT *disguised as a*
TRADER.

TRADER.

Son of Achilles, I found this man on guard,
With two others, beside your ship. I asked him
To tell me where you were, to bring me here.
It was a lucky accident that I found you.
That I happened to anchor here in this bay.

I am the captain of a small merchant-ship.
I am sailing from Troy to Peparethos
To pick up a cargo of wine. When this man said
That he and the others were sailors of yours,   550
I decided to come and tell you the news –
As much as I know – news you may thank me for.

Of course, I could have sailed on without a word.
But you know nothing of what is happening,
What the Greek generals are planning to do –
No, more than planning: what they are doing now.

NEOPTOLEMOS.

Thank you for your kindness, sir. I'll not
Be ungrateful. What is it? What is your news?   560

TRADER.
>They are sending warships to fetch you back.
>Phoinix is in command, and Theseus' sons.

NEOPTOLEMOS.
>To fetch me back? By persuasion, or force?

TRADER.
>My lord, I can't say. I've told you all I know.

NEOPTOLEMOS.
>Phoinix, and Theseus' sons. The orders came
>From the generals themselves, the sons of Atreus?

TRADER.
>My lord, they're on their way. They'll soon be here.

NEOPTOLEMOS.
>Where was Odysseus? Why was he so slow
>To volunteer? He can't have been afraid!

TRADER.
570 >When I left port, he had already sailed
>With Diomedes, to fetch another man.

NEOPTOLEMOS.
>Oh yes? And who has Odysseus gone to fetch?

TRADER.
>His name was – no! Wait! Who is that man there?
>Lower your voice; whisper. Don't let him hear.

NEOPTOLEMOS.
>He is the famous Philoctetes, son of Poias.

TRADER.
>No more, then! Ask me no more! Get clear away
>From the island. Get clear while you still can!

PHILOCTETES.
>Neoptolemos, what is it? Who is this man?
>What are you bargaining behind my back?

NEOPTOLEMOS.
580 >He has more to say. And whatever it is,
>He can say it openly, for us both to hear.

TRADER.
    No, Neoptolemos! I'm a poor man, sir;
    I make my living supplying the army;
    If you tell them . . . if they get to hear of it . . .

NEOPTOLEMOS.
    I am the sworn enemy of the sons of Atreus.
    He hates them too, and therefore is my friend.
    You came to do me a kindness. Do it, then:
    Don't hide what you know. Tell us everything.

TRADER.
    Take care, my lord.

NEOPTOLEMOS.
    I'm not afraid of them.

TRADER.
    It was your own choice.

NEOPTOLEMOS.
    It was my own choice. Speak.   590

TRADER.
    It's this. The two men I told you of,
    Lord Odysseus and Diomedes son of Tydeus –
    This is the man they have sailed to fetch.
    The whole Greek army heard Odysseus swear
    To bring him back, by persuasion or force.
    He made a solemn promise, before the gods:
    He's sure of himself, more than anyone alive.

NEOPTOLEMOS.
    What made them turn their minds to him,
    The generals, after all these years? How can
    He help them now? They marooned him, banished   600
        him –
    What do they want with him now? Have the gods
    Who punish wickedness stirred them at last?

TRADER.
    I'll tell you, everything as it happened.
    There was a noble prophet, Helenus,
    Son of King Priam of Troy. One dark night

The man no good is ever spoken of,
Odysseus, went out alone and captured him
By trickery. A glittering prize! He brought
Him back, and showed him to all the Greeks.

610 Then Helenus began to prophesy.
Of all the things he told them, this was the first:
The city of Troy, he said, would never be theirs
Unless they could persuade this man, Philoctetes,
To leave the island and go back to them.

When he heard that, Odysseus said at once
That he was the man to do it: he would fetch
Philoctetes back, and parade him there
For everyone to see. He thought the man
Would come back by choice; but if not, he said,
He would bring him by force. And if he failed
He would forfeit his own life, his own neck.

620 There, Neoptolemos, you've heard it all.
I advise you to get away now, at once –
You and anyone else you care about.

PHILOCTETES.
So he's sworn to persuade me back? To parade me
In front of them? Odysseus, the plague of Greece!
If I was dead, a corpse in the underworld,
He'd not persuade me back. He will not now.

TRADER.
Well, that's as may be. I must go back, now,
To my ship. May the gods send you all you need.

Exit TRADER.

PHILOCTETES.
Does he really think he can persuade me back?
Does he think he can gentle me with words
630 Into that ship, back to those Greeks? No!
Sooner than him, I'd listen to the snake
That destroyed me, that poisoned away my foot.
But he'll say anything, dare anything.
Neoptolemos, hurry. He'll soon be here.
A whole ocean must separate our ships.

Let us go, now: haste when the time is right
Eases the journey, brings peace and rest at last.

NEOPTOLEMOS.
No, we must wait for the wind. When it changes
We can sail. It's blowing against us now.   640

PHILOCTETES.
When you're running from danger, all winds help.

NEOPTOLEMOS.
No. It's against us. And against them too.

PHILOCTETES.
Against them? What wind has ever stopped
Pirates, criminals, from hunting their prey?

NEOPTOLEMOS.
If that's what you want, we'll sail at once.
Is there anything you need, inside the cave?

PHILOCTETES.
There isn't much – a few necessities.

NEOPTOLEMOS.
Necessities? The ship is well supplied.

PHILOCTETES.
One thing above all: a herb I have found
To poultice the wound and ease the pain.   650

NEOPTOLEMOS.
Go and fetch it, then. Is there anything else?

PHILOCTETES.
The arrows. I must count them, and check that none
Have been left for anyone else to find.

NEOPTOLEMOS.
Is that the famous bow, there in your hand?

PHILOCTETES.
There are no others. Yes, this is the bow.

NEOPTOLEMOS.
May I look at it closer? The bow of the gods!
May I handle it, and pay it my respects?

PHILOCTETES.
> My dear boy, you know that it, and all I have,
> Are at your service. You have only to ask.

NEOPTOLEMOS.
660
> Only to ask . . . If what I want is right
> In the eyes of the gods, I'll ask for it.
> But if it's wrong – well then, let it go.

PHILOCTETES.
> You're right to respect the gods. What you ask
> Is allowed. You have given me back my life;
> You are taking me home to my native land,
> To my dear father and the friends I love;
> My enemies trampled me – you have raised me up.

> Take the bow. Touch it, handle it. Now
> Give it back. There. Now you can boast
> That you and I are the only living men
> To touch it. It is a reward for kindness:
670
> My kindness to another, and now yours to me.

NEOPTOLEMOS.
> My dear friend, thank you. A man who understands
> How to reward kindness with kindness – that man
> Is a friend beyond price. Now, go inside.

PHILOCTETES.
> Come with me. Help me. Let me lean on your arm.

Exeunt PHILOCTETES *and* NEOPTOLEMOS.

SAILORS.
> One other, one other only,
> Has suffered so:
> Ixion, bound to a wheel of fire.
> He slept with Hera, Zeus' queen,
> And he was punished.
680
> But this man is innocent:
> All his life he has lived
> With justice among the just.
> Why has he deserved such pain?

> How has he endured such pain,

A life of tears, alone
By the breakers on the shore?
There was no one else: no one
To hear the cripple's groans
As the sickness gnawed him;   690
No one to gather soothing herbs
When scalding pus oozed
From his ulcers, his gangrened foot.
He crept, he crawled
Like a helpless child
Torn from its nurse's arms.

When the jaws of his pain
Parted a little, and set him free,
He crept out to look for food.
No seeds were his, no fruits   700
Of the bountiful earth,
Such as industrious farmers
Gather and store.
His was the meagre prey
His bow brought down
To feed his belly then.   710

First hunger, then thirst:
For ten long years
No taste of the wine
That brings us joy.
Instead, when he spied
A stagnant pool,
He stooped and drank.

Now he has met, at last,
A man of honour   720
Who will lift him up
To his old, high place.
In a fast ship
Butting the waves
He will take him home.

Home! Where nymphs play
By the river banks

Of Spercheius, and above
On the high hills
Heracles rules,
A man made god
In holy fire.

NEOPTOLEMOS *and* PHILOCTETES *re-enter.*

NEOPTOLEMOS.
730 Come on. Hurry. Why are you standing there dumb?
You're like a man thunderstruck. What's happened?

PHILOCTETES.
Oh!

NEOPTOLEMOS.
What is it?

PHILOCTETES.
It's all right. Go ahead, child.

NEOPTOLEMOS.
Is it the old agony, the old wound?

PHILOCTETES.
No, no. It's all right. It's better now.
O gods!

NEOPTOLEMOS.
Why are you groaning, and calling on the gods?

PHILOCTETES.
O gods, help me. Help me, heal me now.
Ah!

NEOPTOLEMOS.
740 What's the matter? Tell me. If you're in such pain
Tell me. What reason is there for hiding it?

PHILOCTETES.
You're right. There's no use hiding it.
I'm on the rack, Neoptolemos. The pain
Twists . . . gouges . . . tears me alive. O my child . . .
Neoptolemos, I beg you, in the name of god,
Draw your sword, if you have it. Cut, here . . .

Cut off this foot . . . even if I die of it . . .
Neoptolemos, please . . .   750

NEOPTOLEMOS.
This agony, so suddenly – these groans and cries –
Is it some new attack? What has brought it on?

PHILOCTETES.
O my boy . . .

NEOPTOLEMOS.
Yes?

PHILOCTETES.
My boy, my child . . .

NEOPTOLEMOS.
What is it?

PHILOCTETES.
Can't you see? Can't you understand?

NEOPTOLEMOS.
I see how it tortures you.

PHILOCTETES.
Tortures me . . . destroys me. Help me . . . Oh help me.

NEOPTOLEMOS.
How?

PHILOCTETES.
Don't leave me. Don't leave me. Don't be afraid.
The pain . . . this attack . . . the Fury settles here
From time to time . . . on me . . . then someone else . . .

NEOPTOLEMOS.
Philoctetes, I pity you.
I see your suffering, and pity you.   760
How shall I help? Shall I lift you up?

PHILOCTETES.
No. What you asked for before. Take my bow.
Take it. While the pain lasts. Keep it safe for me.
When the attack passes, I fall asleep.
The first sign that it's over. Leave me to sleep,

Don't wake me. If . . . those other men come . . .
770   Neoptolemos, I order you in the name of the gods,
Don't give them the bow, don't let them take it.
If you do, we both die. You murder us both,
Yourself and the man you have sworn to help.

NEOPTOLEMOS.
It's all right. I'll see to it. No one but you
Or I will touch it. Give it me. Pray for good luck.

PHILOCTETES.
There it is, child. Pray to the jealous gods
That they spare you pain such as they have given me,
Suffering like Heracles', who gave me the bow.

NEOPTOLEMOS.
God grant these prayers. And grant us, O god,
780   An easy voyage with a following wind,
Safe journey, wherever our fate is leading us.

PHILOCTETES.
No, child, no. Look! Prayers are useless . . .
Wasted . . . Look! There, inside . . . fresh blood, fresh
   pus
Oozing . . . Oh, it's here again . . . Oh! Oh!
My foot . . . my jailer, my executioner . . .
It's here, it's here . . .
Oh! Oh!

790   Don't leave me . . .

If this were you,
Odysseus . . . if it were only you
Transfixed by this agony . . . Oh! Oh!
If only the generals . . . Agamemnon, Menelaus . . .
The sons of Atreus . . . this should be their pain . . .
Now, forever. Oh! Oh!

O death, I have called you so often –
Come down for me now. Why will you not come?
O my child, O Neoptolemos . . . my boy . . .
The fire, look! Be kind . . . pick me up, and burn me
To ashes . . . a funeral pyre. Then they will call me

The Lemnian. Please, Neoptolemos! Once I, too,   800
Did that kindness for Heracles, son of Zeus . . .
A kindness, a favour . . . he gave me the bow . . .
He gave me the bow for it . . . it's in your hands . . .
O Neoptolemos, answer . . .
Neoptolemos . . . Neoptolemos . . . what is it?

NEOPTOLEMOS.
I suffer for your suffering, in pain for your pain.

PHILOCTETES.
Be comforted. The Fury settles a little
And then flies on. It's not long. Don't leave me . . .

NEOPTOLEMOS.
It's all right. I'll stay. There's no doubt of that.

PHILOCTETES.
In god's name, swear! No: I mustn't ask that.

NEOPTOLEMOS.
They won't let me go without you.   810

PHILOCTETES.
My son . . . your hand . . .

NEOPTOLEMOS.
There. I'll stay.

PHILOCTETES.
Lift me up . . .

NEOPTOLEMOS.
Where?

PHILOCTETES.
Up there.

NEOPTOLEMOS.
It's empty sky. What are you looking at?

PHILOCTETES.
Let me go! Let me go!

NEOPTOLEMOS.
What is it?

PHILOCTETES.
Don't touch me! I'm dying. Don't touch me!

NEOPTOLEMOS.
Calm . . . calm . . . There.

PHILOCTETES.
O earth, mother earth, receive me. I'm dying.
I'll never stand up again. Twisted . . . a
820   cripple . . . sick . . .

NEOPTOLEMOS.
His head is drooping. Soon, he will sleep.
He's covered in sweat; a dark trickle
Of clean blood is running from his foot.
Leave him now. Leave him to sleep in peace.

SAILORS.
Sleep that knows no pain,
No suffering, answer our prayers.
Breathe over us, blessed lord.
830   His eyes are closed:
Breathe over him rest and peace.
Come, sleep, and heal his pain.

FIRST SAILOR.
Now, sir, see where you stand.
What's to be done? What plan
Is best? The man's asleep:
What are we waiting for?
We know what to do –
We must do it, now.

NEOPTOLEMOS.
He can't hear us. The bow is a glittering prize –
840   But without him, if we sail without him, it's nothing.
His is the crown; the gods say he must be fetched;
How can we leave it half-done – and that half by lies?

FIRST SAILOR.
Sir, you must leave that to the gods.
And, sir, you must speak softly,
You must whisper what you say.

For a sick man's sleep
Is restless, easily disturbed –
Quick to hear, and start awake.

SECOND SAILOR.
Now, sir, now it's time.
You must do what must be done.
Finish it! Win the game!   850
Think, sir, and you'll see
That the plan in your mind,
The other plan, will fail.

THIRD SAILOR.
The wind's behind us, sir.
He can see nothing, do nothing –
Stretched out, asleep in the sun.
He doesn't move: hands, feet still.   860
You might think he was dead.
Sir, now it's time.
No risk, no fear –
Surely it's time.

NEOPTOLEMOS.
Be quiet! Fool! Look: he's stirring.
He's opening his eyes. He's awake.

PHILOCTETES.
Bright sunlight . . . I've been asleep. And you . . .
My friends . . . you waited, against all hope.
My son . . . my dear boy . . . I'd never have dared hope
That you'd feel such pity, such friendly care . . .
That you'd wait, and help. The noble generals,   870
The sons of Atreus, were not so long-suffering.

You're a fine boy, the son of a noble father,
And so you put up with it: the groaning,
The smell, everything. You put up with it.

And now the attack is over. The pain has gone,
And the gods have given me a little rest.
Lift me up, Neoptolemos, lift me up.
When the dizziness clears and I can walk,   880
We'll go to the ship, and set sail at once.

NEOPTOLEMOS.
So ill, and so soon recovered! My dear friend,
I'm glad. You were so tortured, at the height
Of the attack, I thought you were sure to die.
Let me help you up. Or else, if you prefer,
My men will carry you: they'll do as we say.

PHILOCTETES.
Neoptolemos, thank you. Help me up:
890   I'll walk. I'll not trouble them yet. The smell
Of my wound will be enough to bear on board.

NEOPTOLEMOS.
Just as you say. Stand up . . . take hold of my
    arm.

PHILOCTETES.
I think I'll be able to stand again . . . There.

NEOPTOLEMOS.
O Zeus! How can I bear it! What shall I do?

PHILOCTETES.
Neoptolemos, what is it? What do you mean?

NEOPTOLEMOS.
How can I tell you? How can I explain?

PHILOCTETES.
Explain what? I don't understand.

NEOPTOLEMOS.
There's no more choice. You must be told.

PHILOCTETES.
900   Must be told what? Is my sickness so foul,
So corrupt, that you're leaving me behind?

NEOPTOLEMOS.
The corruptness, the foulness, are here in me.
I chose to do wrong. I betrayed myself.

PHILOCTETES.
You helped a man who needed help. So like
Your father! How have you betrayed yourself?

NEOPTOLEMOS.
  I chose to do wrong. Soon you'll understand.

PHILOCTETES.
  All you've done is good. Your words make me afraid.

NEOPTOLEMOS.
  Zeus, what can I do? To be a traitor, twice!
  Shall I say nothing and hide it – or tell more lies?

PHILOCTETES.
  Neoptolemos! Surely you don't intend   910
  To leave me here, to leave me and sail away?

NEOPTOLEMOS.
  If only I could! You have to come with me.
  That's the truth, that's the torment I have to bear.

PHILOCTETES.
  What do you mean, child? I still don't understand.

NEOPTOLEMOS.
  Listen, then. It's this. You must sail back to Troy,
  To the Greeks, to the army of the sons of Atreus . . .

PHILOCTETES.
  It's not true! It must be a lie!

NEOPTOLEMOS.
  It's true. But listen . . . let me explain . . .

PHILOCTETES.
  What else have you planned for me?

NEOPTOLEMOS.
  My orders are these: to rescue you from here
  And take you back to sack the land of Troy.   920

PHILOCTETES.
  And that's why you came here?

NEOPTOLEMOS.
  Philoctetes, I had no choice.

PHILOCTETES.
  No choice? Murderer! Stranger! Give me the bow!

NEOPTOLEMOS.
    I have my orders. I must obey.

PHILOCTETES.
    No fire, no monster of hell, no foul scheme
    Festering in the mind, is worse than you.
    You tricked me, you cheated me. The man you helped,
930   The man who trusted you. Trusted you – for this!

    You've stolen my bow, my life. I beg you,
    On my knees I beg you, give it back.
    By the gods you hold dear, give me back my life.

    No. He'll not answer. He turns away.
    He'll not give it back.

    O rocks, hills, lairs of the mountain beasts,
    Harbours and headlands, I cry aloud to you.
    There's no one else. Hear me! Hear me!
940   Hear what Achilles' son has done to me.

    He swore he'd take me home – he's taking me
    To Troy. He held out his hand – and took my bow,
    My sacred bow, the gift of Heracles son of Zeus.
    He wants to brandish it in front of all
    The Greeks, and boast how he won it, how he captured
      me
    In all my strength. He has overpowered a ghost,
    A shadow, an empty husk. And even so
    He could only win by trickery. If I'd had
    My former strength, he'd never have taken me.

    You tricked me, destroyed me. What shall I do?
950   Give it back. I beg you, give it back . . .
    Be your own true self again. My boy, my child . . .

    Still he won't answer. Still he looks away.
    Now I've nothing. O my cave, my double cave,
    Your dear master's here, unarmed, alone.
    I'll come inside; I'll wither and die.
    No birds on the wing, no mountain beasts, will fall
    To these arrows now. I'll die, alone,
    A feast of flesh for the ones I feasted on,

The prey of my prey, my blood for their blood.

He seemed so honest, so innocent of guilt.   960
I trusted him, and he took my life away.

Will you change your mind? Will you pity me?
Then die in misery! Die a traitor's death!

FIRST SAILOR.
Sir, what shall we do? You must decide.
Shall we do as he begs us, or sail for Troy?

NEOPTOLEMOS.
I'm filled with a strange kind of pity.
Ever since I met him, I've pitied him.

PHILOCTETES.
Have mercy, my child. In god's name, pity me.
Who'll honour you for trickery and lies?

NEOPTOLEMOS.
What shall I do? What choice is left for me?
Why did I leave Scyros, and sail for Troy?   970

PHILOCTETES.
You're not wicked: you were trained in wickedness
By those others, those criminals. Leave it to them!
Give me my bow, and sail away from here.

NEOPTOLEMOS (to the FIRST SAILOR).
What do you think, friend? What's your advice?

   Enter ODYSSEUS.

ODYSSEUS.
Traitor! Coward! Give me the bow!

PHILOCTETES.
Odysseus! Is it Odysseus?

ODYSSEUS.
Odysseus, yes.   980

PHILOCTETES.
Then I'm betrayed, I'm dead. You plotted this:
This trickery was yours, to steal the bow.

ODYSSEUS.
Of course. The whole plan, every detail, was mine.

PHILOCTETES.
Boy! Quickly! The bow! Give me the bow!

ODYSSEUS.
He can't, whether he wants to or not. And where
The bow goes, you go. My men will see to that.

PHILOCTETES.
Your men? Have you sunk so low?
Have you brought soldiers here, to lay hands on *me*?

ODYSSEUS.
They're waiting. Will you come willingly, or not?

PHILOCTETES.
In the name of Lemnos, forged by the hand of
      god!
Am I a prisoner, to be dragged away by force?

ODYSSEUS.
Zeus is in command here, Zeus king of the gods.
990   I'm only his servant. This is his will.

PHILOCTETES.
Will you try to make Zeus your accomplice now?
Must he protect you? Must he lie for you?

ODYSSEUS.
Zeus does not lie. He commands. We must obey.

PHILOCTETES.
I won't go.

ODYSSEUS.
You must. There is no other choice.

PHILOCTETES.
O Zeus, was it for this that I was born?
Philoctetes son of Poias – to be a slave?

ODYSSEUS.
Not so. You're not a slave. You're brave, among
The brave: Philoctetes, Sacker of Troy.

PHILOCTETES.
    I refuse! Do what you like to me.
    The cliff . . . the headland, the precipice . . .   1000
      let me go!

ODYSSEUS.
    Go? Why?

PHILOCTETES.
    Sooner than give way, I'll throw myself down,
    And smash myself to pieces on the rocks.

ODYSSEUS.
    Hold him, two of you. Don't let him escape.

PHILOCTETES.
    Hunted, netted, trapped like an animal
    For want of my dear bow . . . and by Odysseus!
    You can think no decent or honest thought;
    You stole up on me, like a thief in the night;
    You set a trap, and used this boy as bait.

    What made you choose him? I didn't know him,   1010
    He was a stranger. He's like me, not you –
    He believes in justice and honesty. All he did
    Was obey orders, and now he is suffering:
    He betrayed me, and betrayed himself as well.
    He was an innocent child: your serpent's tongue,
    Sharp in the shadows, taught him his trade of lies.

    And now you want *me*! You marooned me here
    Alone; you deserted me; you left me to die –
    And now you come back, to drag me away in chains.

    Die! Die by the gods!
    I have prayed that prayer so often. But the gods
    Are deaf. You live and laugh. And I am in pain,   1020
    A tortured wretch, lost in a sea of pain –
    While you laugh, you and the sons of Atreus,
    Your masters, the generals of all the Greeks.

    You had to be tricked, *you* had to be forced
    To accept the yoke, to sail with them to Troy.
    I came willingly, *I* sailed with seven ships –

For this! To be robbed, to be thrown aside!
Was it your work or theirs? Each blames the other.
And now what will you do? Where will you take me?
    Why?
1030 I am nothing. To you, I have long been dead.
Have you forgotten my foot? The stench of it?
If I come with you to Troy, how will you pray,
How will you sacrifice? Have you forgotten?
That was your excuse for leaving me here before.

Die! Die in agony!
If the gods are just, die for your crimes to me!
Are they not just? Did they not spur you on
To launch your ship, and sail to fetch me home?

1040 O gods of my native land,
Punish them! Punish them! If you pity me,
If the time is right, rise up and punish them.
My life is torture – but if I see them dead,
If you punish them, I'll think my pain is cured.

FIRST SAILOR.
Stubborn words, Odysseus – stubborn words
From a stubborn man. He'll not give way.

ODYSSEUS.
I could answer him. There are many arguments.
But now is not the time. I'll say just this:
I make myself the man each occasion demands.
1050 When honesty and justice are required,
I am the justest, most honest man alive.
But in everything I do, I fight to win.
Except this once. This once, I give way to you.

Let him go. He's free.
He can stay on the island. We have the bow –
We don't need you. Prince Teucer is with us still,
A skilled bowman – and I am there myself,
As clever as you, I think, at archery.
1060 We don't need you. Stay here! Enjoy your island!

It's time to go. Perhaps this bow, this prize
Of his, will bring me the honour reserved for him.

PHILOCTETES.
    You'll take my bow? You'll take it, and flaunt
    Yourself with it, in front of all the Greeks?

ODYSSEUS.
    There's nothing more to say. It's time to go.

PHILOCTETES.
    Son of Achilles, will you not answer me?
    Will you sail away, and leave me without a word?

ODYSSEUS.
    On, Neoptolemos! So decent, so honest –
    If you once look at him, we lose the game!

PHILOCTETES.
    My friends, pity me. Don't leave me here alone.   1070

FIRST SAILOR.
    We obey his orders. It's for him to say.

NEOPTOLEMOS.
    I know I'll be called soft-hearted, easy.
    But you can do as he asks. You can stay here
    While the ship's prepared, and sacrifice
    Is made for a fair wind. Perhaps he'll change
    His mind; perhaps he'll understand at last.

    Lord Odysseus and I will go on ahead.
    We'll signal when it's time. Come then, at once.   1080

    ODYSSEUS, NEOPTOLEMOS *and their sailors go.*

PHILOCTETES.
    Rock-tomb, rock-womb,
    Sun-warm, ice-cold,
    Home of my misery
    Forever, home
    Till the day I die.
    Weep for me, echo my grief.
    How must I live?
    Where must I turn   1090
    For food, for hope
    To nourish me?

To the birds above?
They fly free
On the wind's wings:
All my strength is gone.

FIRST SAILOR.
You chose this fate;
You burdened yourself.
It was not imposed
By a greater power.
You had a choice,
1100   And you chose this fate.

PHILOCTETES.
Distracted with grief
And torn with pain;
A hermit, stripped
Of all company
Till the day I die.
Stripped of my strength,
1110   The swift arrows
That brought me food.
Dark, twisted words
Choked my mind.
If only that man,
That cunning man,
Shared all my pain,
My endless pain.

FIRST SAILOR.
This is no trick,
Sir: this is fate.
We're not to blame.
1120   Turn your curses away,
Curse someone else.
We're your friends.

PHILOCTETES.
On the shore, by the grey sea,
He sits and laughs at me.
In his hands he waves my bow.
The bow of my life, the bow

That nourished me, the bow
No other man has held but me.

O my dear bow, stolen away
From the loving hands that held you,
If you could see, if you could feel,
How you would pity me: 1130
Heracles' friend, your old master,
Your master no more.

You have a new master now,
New hands to string, to bend, to fire.
Look at his face, and see deceit,
Injustice, treachery – my enemy,
And all the teeming agony
His cunning has made for me.

FIRST SAILOR.
A person should speak only the truth: 1140
No slander, no venom of the tongue.
Odysseus was sent here, one man
By many. He was obeying orders;
What he did was a service,
A service to help his friends.

PHILOCTETES.
Birds of the air; wild beasts,
Eyes gleaming in the hills
Where I hunted you, now you are safe!
Start up from your lairs and flee
No more. My hands are empty,   1150
My weapons, my arrows, gone.

There is no more terror now,
No more danger. The island
Is yours: walk freely
Where you will. Soon
It will be time to feast,
To glut yourselves on my rotting flesh,
My blood for yours.

My life will be over soon.
Soon I will die. For where,
And how, will I find my food?

1160   Can a man eat empty air?
       Mother Earth, who feeds all men,
       Gives me no nourishment.

FIRST SAILOR.
       Come nearer: we are your friends.
       What we say is good advice.
       Remember: it's in your own power
       To change your fate, to rid yourself
       Of this burden of plague,
       This suffering that eats your life.

PHILOCTETES.
1170   Must you torture me still?
       Kindest of friends,
       Must you open the wound
       And torment me still?

FIRST SAILOR.
       What have we done?

PHILOCTETES.
       Why, why did you come?
       Why did you ever hope
       To take me back
       To that detested Troy?

FIRST SAILOR.
       We think it best.

PHILOCTETES.
       Leave me! Leave me now!

FIRST SAILOR.
       Very well. Your words
       Are welcome. Let's go, men:
1180   The ship is waiting.

PHILOCTETES.
       Don't go! In the name
       Of the anger of Zeus, don't go!

FIRST SAILOR.
       Be calm.

PHILOCTETES.
In god's name, wait.

FIRST SAILOR.
For what?

PHILOCTETES.
Pain . . . pain . . .
Demon pain . . .
Twisting, torturing . . .
My foot . . .
How can I bear it?
Why can't I die?
O my friends, come back.   1190

FIRST SAILOR.
Have you changed your mind?
What must we do?

PHILOCTETES.
Don't be angry.
I was delirious.
The jagged pain . . .
I said . . . I didn't mean . . .

FIRST SAILOR.
Come with us. Do as we ask.

PHILOCTETES.
No! Not if Zeus himself
In a flash of white fire
Scorches me, sears me to the bone.
Topple, Troy, and crush them,   1200
My enemies who took me
A cripple, and left me here.
O my friends, my dear friends, if only . . .

FIRST SAILOR.
What do you ask?

PHILOCTETES.
Give me an axe, a sword, a spear . . .

FIRST SAILOR.
What new madness . . . ?

PHILOCTETES.
> Head . . . arms . . . hack them,
> Butcher them . . .
> I must die now.

FIRST SAILOR.
> Why?

PHILOCTETES.
1210
> I must find him . . . my father . . .

FIRST SAILOR.
> Where?

PHILOCTETES.
> In Hades . . . in the underworld,
> Far from this light.
> O my native land,
> If only I could come home . . .
> Cursed, since the day
> I left the holy river, and came
> To the Greeks, my enemies,
> To help them. No more . . . no more . . .

> *Exit* PHILOCTETES.

FIRST SAILOR.
> We should have gone to the ship long ago.
1220
> But here comes Neoptolemos – and Odysseus with
> him.

NEOPTOLEMOS *and* ODYSSEUS *re-enter.*

ODYSSEUS.
> Where are you going? Why are you hurrying back?

NEOPTOLEMOS.
> I did wrong before. Now I must set things right.

ODYSSEUS.
> You're talking nonsense. What wrong did you do?

NEOPTOLEMOS.
> I took orders from you and the other Greeks –

ODYSSEUS.
> And you call that wrong? What was wrong in that?

NEOPTOLEMOS.
I used trickery and lies to cheat a man.

ODYSSEUS.
What do you mean now? What madness is this?

NEOPTOLEMOS.
No madness. A debt. A debt I mean to pay.   1230

ODYSSEUS.
What are you saying? You intend to give – ?

NEOPTOLEMOS.
I intend to give back the bow I stole.

ODYSSEUS.
You can't mean it! To give back the bow – !

NEOPTOLEMOS.
I stole it, and now I intend to give it back.

ODYSSEUS.
Is this a joke? In god's name, is this a joke?

NEOPTOLEMOS.
It's no joke. I mean it. It's the truth.

ODYSSEUS.
You'll really do it?

NEOPTOLEMOS.
Are three times not enough?

ODYSSEUS.
Once was enough.

NEOPTOLEMOS.
Then there's no more to say.   1240

ODYSSEUS.
You won't do it. You'll be stopped.

NEOPTOLEMOS.
Stopped? Who by?

ODYSSEUS.
The soldiers of Greece, and among them me.

NEOPTOLEMOS.
　The wise Odysseus! You talk like a fool.

ODYSSEUS.
　You're the fool, in all you do or say.

NEOPTOLEMOS.
　Fool or not, what I intend is just.

ODYSSEUS.
　Just? To give him back this prize – the prize
　I helped you win?

NEOPTOLEMOS.
　The prize you helped me steal.
　I cheated; I lied. I must set things right.

ODYSSEUS.
1250　Aren't you afraid? The army of the Greeks –

NEOPTOLEMOS.
　My army is justice. *You* should be afraid.

ODYSSEUS.
　And if I use force?

NEOPTOLEMOS.
　My mind's made up.

ODYSSEUS.
　If I forget the Trojans, and fight with *you* . . . ?

NEOPTOLEMOS.
　The choice is made.

ODYSSEUS.
　Here is my sword.

NEOPTOLEMOS.
　And mine. I'm ready. Will you stand, and fight?

ODYSSEUS.
　No, I'll not kill you. I'll go back to them,
　And give them my report. They'll deal with you.

NEOPTOLEMOS.
　Wise Odysseus! Common sense at last!
1260　Remember this, and keep clear of trouble.

ODYSSEUS *goes.*

NEOPTOLEMOS.
  Philoctetes. Philoctetes, son of Poias.

PHILOCTETES.
  Who's there? Who's calling, outside the cave?

  Enter PHILOCTETES.

  Neoptolemos! What evil brings you again?
  Have you brought new pain to top the old?

NEOPTOLEMOS.
  Don't be afraid. Listen. Hear what I say.

PHILOCTETES.
  I listened before. Honeyed words! I listened,
  I trusted you – and you brought me to this!

NEOPTOLEMOS.
  And if I say I've had a change of heart?   1270

PHILOCTETES.
  A change of heart? You were like this before –
  Until you stole my bow. You smiled – and lied.

NEOPTOLEMOS.
  I'm not lying now. I want to ask you this:
  Will you stay here, endure it to the end,
  Or will you sail with us?

PHILOCTETES.
  Enough! You waste words.
  I'll not listen. I'll hear no more arguments.

NEOPTOLEMOS.
  Your mind is fixed?

PHILOCTETES.
  More firmly than you know.

NEOPTOLEMOS.
  If I could have persuaded you, I would.
  But if all my words are wasted –

PHILOCTETES.
  Every one!   1280

You can say nothing that pleases me, nothing
I want to hear. You stole my life, my bow –
And now you bring me arguments instead!
That Prince Achilles should father such a son!
Die, all of you! The sons of Atreus first,
Odysseus next, and last Neoptolemos!

NEOPTOLEMOS.
You can save your curses. Here is your bow.

PHILOCTETES.
What did you say? Is this another lie?

NEOPTOLEMOS.
No lie. I swear by the honour of Zeus himself.

PHILOCTETES.
1290   Words of happiness . . . if only they're true . . .

NEOPTOLEMOS.
They're true. This is the proof. Take your bow.

    ODYSSEUS' *voice is heard from offstage.*

ODYSSEUS.
No! I forbid it, in the name of god!
For the sake of the army, for the sake
Of the sons of Atreus, give me the bow!

PHILOCTETES.
Odysseus! That was Odysseus' voice.

ODYSSEUS (*off*).
Odysseus, yes. And I am here: I have come
To take you by force to the plain of Troy,
Whether Achilles' son agrees, or not.

PHILOCTETES.
One arrow will stop these boasts.

NEOPTOLEMOS.
1300   Philoctetes, no!

PHILOCTETES.
Let me go, boy. In god's name, let me go.

NEOPTOLEMOS.
  I can't.

PHILOCTETES.
  Why did you stop me from killing him –
  My enemy, the man I most hate in Greece?

NEOPTOLEMOS.
  Enemy or friend, he's not for us to kill.

PHILOCTETES.
  I tell you this: those leaders of the Greeks,
  Those glib spokesmen, are brave enough with words,
  But when it comes to fighting they cower, they cringe.

NEOPTOLEMOS.
  He's gone. You have your bow. There's no more cause
  For anger. I helped you: I'm no more to blame.

PHILOCTETES.
  Neoptolemos, son of Achilles, you have shown   1310
  The true spirit of your father, the finest of all
  The heroes of Greece, alive or among the dead.

NEOPTOLEMOS.
  Philoctetes, thank you. You give high praise
  To my father and myself. Give one thing more:
  A fair hearing for what I have to ask.
  All mortals must bear whatever fate the gods
  Allot them, good or bad – but when a man
  Brings suffering on himself, and clings to it
  As you do, no one forgives or pities him.   1320

  You're like a savage; you take no advice;
  When people offers you a friendly word
  You spit with hate, as if they meant you harm.
  Even so, I will speak. In your name, lord Zeus!
  Hear what I say: imprint it on your mind.

  The sickness you are suffering came from a god.
  You strayed inside the sacred shrine of Chryse,
  And disturbed the hidden snake, its guardian.
  And now you are poisoned, you will find no cure
  While the sun sets and rises, rises and sets,   1330
  Until you come to Troy of your own free will.

We have doctors there, sons of Asclepius,
And they will cure your wound. Then, with this bow,
And my help, you'll topple the towers of Troy.

I'll tell you how I know that this is true.
There's a prisoner in camp, a man of Troy,
The prophet Helenus. He has prophesied
Plainly that all this will happen – and more,
1340   That Troy will fall before this summer ends.
He'll give his life as forfeit if he lies.

You've heard it all. Give way. Do as I ask.
There are rich rewards: to be called a prince
Of princes, to find healing for your wound,
And this above all, to capture tearful Troy.

PHILOCTETES.
Detested life, why do you keep me here
In the world above, and not send me down to Hades?
1350   What can I do? Must I reject his words,
The advice of a true friend – or give way to him?
A sick man, a cripple – if I go back,
How can I face them? What can I say to them?

It's not resentment for the past that stings,
But fear of the future. I understand these men.
Once the first wickedness is hatched, their minds
1360   Breed nothing but wickedness, nothing but crime.

And you, Neoptolemos: I don't understand.
You have every reason to stay away from Troy,
Not to persuade me back. They wronged you, too:
They plundered your father's arms – Achilles' arms! –
And gave them to Odysseus. Must you go back
And fight their battles? Must I fight too?

No, Neoptolemos! Take me home instead;
Go back to Scyros; leave those evil men
To die an evil death. If you help me now
1370   You will earn a double blessing, a double thanks –
Mine and your father's. But if he sees you
Helping those hated men, he'll hate you too.

NEOPTOLEMOS.
I hear what you say. Even so, I beg you:
Trust me, trust the gods. Sail back with me.

PHILOCTETES.
To Troy, to the accursed sons of Atreus?
A helpless cripple – and King Agamemnon?

NEOPTOLEMOS.
To skilful doctors who will heal your foot,
Dry up the ulcers and end your agony.

PHILOCTETES.
Cunning words! You're so full of good advice!   1380

NEOPTOLEMOS.
What I advise is best – for both of us.

PHILOCTETES.
The gods are listening! Are you not ashamed?

NEOPTOLEMOS.
Why should I be ashamed? The advice is good.

PHILOCTETES.
Good for the sons of Atreus, not for me.

NEOPTOLEMOS.
Yes, for you. I'm your friend. I'm helping you.

PHILOCTETES.
You're betraying me, helping my enemies.

NEOPTOLEMOS.
My poor friend, so stubborn, so determined to suffer.

PHILOCTETES.
I hear my death in every word you say.

NEOPTOLEMOS.
You refuse to listen, refuse to understand.

PHILOCTETES.
This much I understand: they marooned me here.   1390

NEOPTOLEMOS.
They marooned you, and now they'll rescue you.

PHILOCTETES.
I'll never agree to go back to Troy.

NEOPTOLEMOS.
What can I do? You've rejected all
My arguments. Perhaps I should leave you here,
Without more words, to live the life you live
Here on the island, with no one to rescue you.

PHILOCTETES.
If it has to be endured, I'll endure it.
But remember your promise, Neoptolemos:
1400   Your promise to take me home. Oh, do it now!
Forget Troy. We've had pain and tears enough.

NEOPTOLEMOS.
I agree. Let's go.

PHILOCTETES.
Neoptolemos . . . you agree?

NEOPTOLEMOS.
Walk with firm steps.

PHILOCTETES.
As firmly as I can.

NEOPTOLEMOS.
The Greeks will punish me.

PHILOCTETES.
Pay them no heed.

NEOPTOLEMOS.
If they attack my country . . . ?

PHILOCTETES.
1410   I will be there.

NEOPTOLEMOS.
How will you help?

PHILOCTETES.
With the arrows of Heracles.

NEOPTOLEMOS.
You mean . . . ?

PHILOCTETES.
  I will drive them away.

NEOPTOLEMOS.
  My true friend! My ally!
  Kiss Lemnos farewell; come to the ship.

  The god HERACLES *enters above.*

HERACLES.
  Stop! Philoctetes, son of Poias,
  Listen to my words.   1420
  You hear, you see,
  Heracles son of Zeus.
  From the high place
  Of Olympos I have come down
  To tell you the will of Zeus
  And prevent this journey.
  Hear me. Hear me now.

  Remember my story: my twelve labours,
  And my reward, this immortality.
  For you, too, there are labours to perform: 1430
  For you, too, the rewards are glory and fame.

  You will go back with this man to the towers of Troy;
  You will find doctors there, to heal your wound;
  You will be chosen champion of all the Greeks –
  And with this bow, my gift, you will kill
  Paris of Troy, who caused this suffering.
  You will plunder his city, and carry home
  Rich tribute, the prize of the battlefield:
  Home to Poias your father and your native land.   1440

  Son of Achilles, my words are for your ears too.
  Without his help, you will never topple Troy;
  Without your help, he too must fall. For you
  Are like lions, a pair of lions, joined in the hunt.

  I will send doctors to Troy to heal his wound.
  The city is doomed to fall, twice, to this bow.
  And when you plunder Troy remember this,   1450
  This above all: true reverence for the gods.

For nothing is greater in the sight of Zeus
Than reverence. It lives in all men's hearts.
They are mortal, they die; but reverence never dies.

PHILOCTETES.
O voice of god; dear friend
I longed to see again –
I hear, I will obey.

NEOPTOLEMOS.
I, too, hear and obey.

HERACLES.
Lose no more time.
1460   The hour and tide of fate
Are with you. The moment is now.

    Exit HERACLES.

PHILOCTETES.
It is time to say a last farewell
To the cave that watched with me;
The spirits of brooks and fields
And the deep, full-throated roar
Where waves boom on the high cliffs;
My cave-shelter, wet with spray
Borne on the driving wind;
The Hill of Hermes, echoing
1470   My tears, my wintry grief.
It is time to leave the pools,
The bubbling streams; time to take
The unlooked-for gift of fate.
O Lemnos, my island, smile on me,
Send me safe sailing; I go
Where great Destiny leads, my friends'
Advice, and the all-powerful god
Who chose what has happened here.

SAILORS.
Gather now, and pray
1480   To the spirits of the sea
To lead us safely home.

    Exeunt OMNES.

A Note on the Translators and Series Editor

ROBERT CANNON is Vice-Principal of the Rose Bruford College of Speech and Drama where he has helped pioneer unique degrees in training for the professional theatre. His performed translations include *Hippolytos* and *Trojan Women* by Euripides, *The New House* by Goldoni and *Antigone* (and the accompanying *Model Book*) by Brecht. Other work includes verse translations of Leopardi and Foscolo as well as articles on Stanislavski and the opera, the Elizabethan theatre and aspects of the Talmud. He has written several plays, one of which, *Anna Petrovna* was included in the Royal Shakespeare Company's season 'Undiscovered Country'.

KENNETH McLEISH's translations, of plays by all the Greek and Roman dramatists, Ibsen, Feydeau, Molière, Strindberg and others, have been performed throughout the world on stage, film, TV and radio. His original plays include *I Will If You Will*, *Just Do It*, *The Arabian Nights*, *Omma* and *Orpheus*. His books include *The Theatre of Aristophanes*, *Guide to Shakespeare's Plays* (with Stephen Unwin), *The Good Reading Guide* and *Guide to Greek Theatre and Drama*. He was editor of the Drama Classics series for Nick Hern Books and a Fellow of the Royal Society of Literature.

J. MICHAEL WALTON worked in the professional theatre as an actor and director before joining the University of Hull, where he is Professor of Drama. He has published four books on Greek theatre, *Greek Theatre Practice*, *The Greek Sense of Theatre: Tragedy Reviewed*, *Living Greek Theatre: A Handbook of Classical Performance and Modern Production* and *Menander and the Making of Comedy* (with the late Peter Arnott). He edited *Craig on Theatre* for Methuen and is Series Editor of Methuen Classical Greek Dramatists. He has translated plays by Sophocles, Euripides, Menander and Terence and is Director of the Performance Translation Centre in the drama Department at the University of Hull.

Companies, institutions and other organisations wishing to make bulk purchases of any Methuen Drama books published by Random House should contact their local bookseller or Random House direct: Product Manager, Methuen Drama, Random House UK Ltd, 20 Vauxhall Bridge Road, London SW1V 2SA. Tel: 0171 840 8400; Fax: 0171 834 2509. For a FREE Methuen Drama catalogue please contact Methuen Drama at the Above address.